DESTROYING THE ROOT of RACISM

Library of Congress Control Number: 2015955174

ISBN: 978-1-63308-183-3 Hardback
          978-1-63308-184-0 Paperback
          978-1-63308-185-7 Digital

Interior and Cover Design by R'tor John D. Maghuyop

 CHALFANT ECKERT
PUBLISHING

1028 S Bishop Avenue, Dept. 178
Rolla, MO 65401

Printed in United States of America

DESTROYING THE ROOT of RACISM

DR. RON WEBB

CHALFANT ECKERT

PUBLISHING

TABLE OF CONTENTS

FOREWORD

I t is with great enthusiasm and without reservation that I invite you to glean wisdom from the pages of Bishop Webb's new book, *Destroying the Root of Racism*. Written for such a time as this, Dr. Webb brings God front and center on every page and shines a light into our racially-motivated dark places so that we can see our fellow man of any ethnic or racial heritage as God does, co-heir with Christ and a child of the Most High God.

Bishop Webb doesn't excuse the church from responsibility for the ongoing racial violence and tension that surrounds many urban areas in the United States. Not dwelling on the negative, he presents a powerful message of standing up, stepping out of our comfort zones, and being on the front lines of restoration to aid those who have been damaged emotionally and spiritually by the cruelty of racism and prejudice.

In the tradition of his last written masterpiece, *Leadership From Behind the Scenes*, prepare to be WOWed by the simplicity and thoroughness of the solution Bishop Webb presents to the Body of Christ to erase racism from our culture in this generation.

Dr. Kitty Bickford, DBS, CPC
Founder, Pasture Valley Children Missions
Author, *Nonprofit Touchdown*
and *Do Your Own Nonprofit* series

ACKNOWLEDGMENTS

This is one of the most difficult parts of writing any book – the acknowledgments. There are so many people who played a major part in making this book a reality. I'm so thankful that God placed such wonderful people in my path who have encouraged me, inspired me, prayed for me, and spoke wisdom into my life. I am so fortunate to have so many good friends, it would be impossible to list them all without leaving someone out, so instead I will say thank you to all of the special people in my life that have impacted my life.

To my wife Georgia, thanks for your patience and support in my writing this book. And thank you my children Ronnie, Jackie (Jerrell, Sr.), Tony (Ramona), and two of the greatest grandsons in the world, Jerrell, Jr. and Jaxson. To my incredible staff and advisors, Dave, Jackie, Jamie, and Jeanne: Thank you for all you do. My dear friends who are in an elite category and demand special mention include Dr. John Hagler, whose friendship has been filled with deep and transparent conversations – thank you for your honesty. Special thanks to the late and great Alfonse Webb, Sr., and my very special mother who raised ten kids to love, honor, and respect those in authority.

Thank you, Benny Robertson, for your willingness to listen and share your heart on this sensitive matter, you are a great friend. To all my pastor friends who believe in the unity of spirit who will not allow race to divide us, thank you for taking a stand.

INTRODUCTION

As I set out to write this book, I felt somewhat like the Apostle Paul as he wrote a letter to the church at Corinth. He said, *"For out of much affliction and anguish of heart I wrote unto you with many tears; not that ye should be grieved, but that ye might know the love which I have more abundantly unto you."* (2 Corinthians 2:4). When I observe the way this painful spirit of racism is tearing apart not only our country but the church as well, my heart breaks. However, this time was predicted in the Bible.

> *"And ye shall hear of wars and rumors of wars:*
> *see that ye be not troubled: for all these things must*
> *come to pass, but the end is not yet. For nation shall*
> *rise against nation, and kingdom against kingdom: and*
> *there shall be famines, and pestilences, and earthquakes,*
> *in diverse places. All these are the beginning of sorrows.*
> *Then shall they deliver you up to be afflicted, and*
> *shall kill you: and ye shall be hated of all nations for*
> *my name's sake. And then shall many be offended, and*
> *shall betray one another, and shall hate one another."*
>
> –Matthew 24:6-10

Nation shall rise against nation. In other words, different ethnic groups or groups of people against one another. This racial divide makes my heart sick, especially when I see it in the Body of Christ. While there is so much I could write about in terms of racism, this book is not to cast a bad light on any specific race. Though I will be sharing a few of my personal stories, keep in mind that I'm not writing from my own perspective, but from a Biblical one.

I'm sure many of you have suffered from this demonic spirit of racism because all demonic spirits need a willing vessel. It's like a cancer, growing and spreading until it infiltrates every facet of our lives, down to the very structure of our society. This cultural cancer seems nearly impossible to overcome. Seminars, meetings, speeches—none of them seem to be making a difference. Even when the issue of racism is addressed, it only leads to more anger and frustration. Why is that? Because the world continues to see race as a problem of skin color. My friend, RACISM HAS NEVER BEEN A SKIN PROBLEM. IT IS A SIN PROBLEM!

We hear of so much violence in our country today through shootings and shedding of innocent blood. Lives end prematurely, and it seems as though there's no end to it. The June 25, 2015 South Carolina shooting is a perfect example. Nine innocent lives were taken when a disturbed young man turned a gun on the members of a Bible study he was attending. Though the church members posed no threat to the man, he killed them one by one because of the color of their skin. And all of this before our nation had recovered from previous racial tragedies such as the November, 2014 unrest in Ferguson, Missouri.

In light of these violent acts, many call for the removal of a flag as the solution. However, removing a flag doesn't remove the hatred from people's hearts. As I've often said, racism in not a skin problem, it's a sin problem, an issue of the heart. Why are we as Christians sitting back and hoping the justice system will work it out? Our justice system, in its flawed state, is no match for the situation at hand. Without God, there will be no resolution.

Whether you are Black, White, Asian, Indian, Hispanic, Arab or any other race, your life is important. It is a tragedy when anyone's life ends prematurely, especially when it is due to violence. It breaks my heart anytime I hear of an unlawful death. No family should have to go through that kind of pain, regardless of their race, gender, or social status. It's a tragedy.

So instead of focusing on one particular race, we should hold all lives as important and valuable. Each person was created by our Heavenly Father. Each of us is precious to Him, handcrafted for a specific purpose. So, going forward, let's treat one another like the treasures that we are. Let's remember that all life is worth protecting. Every life matters.

Now, having recited just a few of the issues, let me present a solution. First of all, it's unfair to judge an entire race based on the actions of a few people. To say all black people are the same, or all white, Hispanic, or Asian people are the same is simply untrue and unjust. Just because people may disagree with you on certain issues, it doesn't necessarily mean they are racist. I have white friends who make statements about black people whom I love, but it doesn't make them racist. The same can be said of my black friends who make comments about white people; they're not racist.

It's sad we all have to walk on eggshells around one another. We shouldn't have to be afraid that something we say may be taken wrong and cause offense. Granted, racism is a sensitive subject. However, we should approach it with open hearts and open minds, and hear the other person out before you form an opinion about them.

Pointing fingers and disrespecting or trying to belittle people of another race will never make anything better. It takes sensible, level-headed people sitting down with open hearts and determination to resolve this issue.

Before we can begin to build a bridge between the races, we must first examine ourselves. Is there hatred and racism in our own lives? The answer may be more complicated than you think. Racism can take many forms. It can be seen, as in cases in which violence and verbal abuse are present, or unseen, where the sin occurs in the heart and mind without any outward sign.

As Christians it is imperative that we constantly examine ourselves, checking our thoughts and actions against the Word of God so we don't fall prey to this trap. 1 Corinthians 13:5 says it like this:

> *"Examine and test and evaluate your own selves to see whether you are holding to your faith and showing the proper fruits of it. Test and prove yourselves. Do you not yourselves realize and know thoroughly by an ever-increasing experience that Jesus Christ is in you—unless you are counterfeits disapproved on trial and rejected?"* AMP

Maybe you've never been mean or degrading to a person of another race but have judged them in your mind. Or perhaps you hate those whose race is different from your own, though you never speak your hatred aloud. Whether or not there is a physical manifestation, it's still sin. The Bible tells us in 1 Samuel 16:7:

"For the Lord seeth not as man seeth; for man looketh on the outward appearance, but the Lord looketh on the heart."

However, before we even begin this discussion, you need to understand that racism is not a one-way street. Whether you're white and hate blacks, black and hate whites, Hispanic and hate Asians, or Indian and hate Arabs, the bottom line is that if you have negative feelings toward other people based on their skin color or nationality, then you are engaging in racism.

I'm just simply telling it how it is. No matter what race you are, racism is a sin. All too often, it's a sin that goes unchallenged. I applaud those individuals who will stand off in the face of adversity and speak out against this immoral behavior. It takes great courage to stand up for what is right.

Regardless of your racial background or social status, it's much easier to go about your life as if nothing is wrong, as if you don't recognize this sickness that has taken over our world.

While we hide behind our church doors, our enemy gains strength. It's time we come out of the shadows and fight this demon called racism. I know it's not the easy choice, but it's the right choice.

Now here's the hard part, but bear with me. It's not the world that needs reprimanding, but the church. In this book, I want to focus on what the church, and more specifically, its leaders should be doing. As a body we have been silent on the issue of racism for far too long. We want to let someone else handle tough situations and only speak up after the fact. The Church is supposed to be the light of the world, but our light has gone very dim. It's our place to lead the way. We should be the first to forgive and apologize, the first to help and support those around us. Let's come together in unity to show the world what the love of God truly is.

Join me as we journey through this book. I will outline the issues surrounding racism and present Biblical solutions. It's my sincere prayer that this book will open the eyes of our leaders, both Christian and secular, so that together we can make a stand for the just and right cause. We, together with God, can rip out the roots of racism in our country. Together we can bring about a change in our world.

Bishop Ron Webb

CHAPTER 1

THE BLAME GAME

The subject of race has become a volatile topic in our nation of late. Just mentioning it stirs up such pain and resentment, it breaks my heart. Something that should be the glue that bind us together has become a vehicle for violence. Whether directly or indirectly, this issue has affected millions in our world in the past and present, and will continue to affect future lives. Those who have been victims of racism or have had to deal with the repercussions of it; they want justice and are looking for somewhere to place the blame. Unfortunately, that blame is often misplaced, and fingers are pointed in the wrong direction.

There have been countless times in my life when I've been mistreated or discriminated against because of my skin color. I understand the want for justice and recompense. However, as I have come to learn, the only thing accomplished by placing the blame on someone is prolonging the pain. Why?

Because Satan is the real enemy here, all the blame goes to him. Trying to make people accountable for your pain will only serve to further the enemy's agenda. It's his ultimate goal to keep you from God. The Bible calls Satan the *father of lies.* (John 8:44). His deception causes people to buy into the idea of racism, even though it's scientifically unsound.

> *"For where envying and strife is, there is confusion and every evil work."*
>
> –James 3:16

By allowing Satan to draw you into conflict and strife, you are inviting confusion into your life. He is constantly trying to disrupt the plan God has for your life, and distraction is one of his many tools. If you're busy focusing on the people you perceive to be the enemy, you take your eyes off of God. And when you're no longer focusing on God, the enemy can wreak havoc in your life. Don't let Satan pull you into this trap. Remember, he's the real enemy.

Unfortunately, the Church has fallen short in this area. We've let the enemy run amok far too long. Now we've come to a point of action. The violence is spreading; it's not just an urban problem anymore. Hate groups are now more active than ever.

But where is the Church in all of this? We should be the referees, keeping the peace and maintaining order. Yet no one is blowing the whistle. Instead, we only add to the chaos and disorder.

I remember hearing about the 2005 levee break in New Orleans. The levee was designed to hold back the floodwaters and keep the people safe. However, when it failed, thousands of homes were flooded and many people died.

The Church is a levee. We were designed to protect the people, but right now we're broken and our people are sinking. We've failed them. It's time we stop pointing fingers and work together to help heal our nation. Let's step out and reveal the real enemy. Instead of trying to find someone to blame for the problem, let's work together on the solution.

CHAPTER 2

A CALL TO RIGHT THE WRONG

Racism is quickly becoming the most prevalent issue in our nation. And our nation isn't the only one suffering; it is a significant, worldwide problem. We see it in the news every day and hear about it on the radio. It seems to be an ever-increasing crisis. Left unchecked and unchanged, it can and will develop into something far worse. We're standing on a precipice, called to a point of action. Now, more than ever, the world needs the Church to stand up and fulfill its purpose. We are called to lead others to reformation and reconciliation. It's time we answer that call.

On a recent trip to the dentist, I learned something that caused me to come to a new realization. I went in to have a root canal procedure done, but the tooth was infected. The dentist explained to me how they had to draw out the infection before they could complete the procedure. Otherwise, when they covered it up with a cap, it would trap the infection inside and cause it to become far worse.

I realized then that the problem of racism is much like a root canal. We have to get down to the root, create change, treat the infection, and get rid of the hurt and pain in the way.

The first step is to draw out the infection. Like with a root canal, a cap can be put over it to make it look pretty. It merely hides the infection underneath, allowing it to fester and grow. This infection sickens and weakens the body. It has to be dealt with, has to be removed before you can start working on the root.

There are two things to remember in dealing with racism. First, there is no easy fix, but it's worth fixing anyway. Second, it will hurt, but only for a moment. In the long run, it's much better for you and the only way to achieve healing.

Racism is the idea that one group of people is superior to another strictly based on color or ethnicity. This belief goes directly against the character of God. The Bible clearly states that we were all made in his image. How then can one race be superior due to physical attributes?

Reports of racism have been around as long as there has been written history: the Jews enslaved by Egyptians, genocide in Africa, Hitler's 'Superior Race', and even now in the United States and in the Middle East, to name a few. Throughout history, race has been a dividing line for humanity. It's driven us apart through violence and chaos, creating pockets of hatred all around the globe. It's a very complex and controversial problem with no quick fix. However, that doesn't mean there isn't any solution.

So, how do we bridge the gap between the races? How do we bring calm to the chaos? With the current state of racial dissension, many look to our government or some other secular avenue for a solution. But the truth is, there is no human resolution. God is the only answer. Why? Because racism isn't a physical issue, it's a spiritual one.

When we dig deeper, down to the root of the problem, we find it stems from a myriad of sins; racism is simply the fruit thereof. You can't plant an apple tree and expect to get peaches from it. If you want a different fruit, you have to change the root. Likewise, if we want to effect change where racism is concerned, we have to start at the origin of the problem. It's time we acknowledge racism for the sin it is and proactively work toward uprooting it.

> *"He that saith he is in the light, and hateth his brother, is in darkness even until now."*
>
> —1 John 2:9

As I said in the introduction, racism has never been a skin problem; it's a sin problem. This is a fact the Church must realize and acknowledge before we can ever move forward toward healing and unity. Many sins are connected with racism, chiefest among them being hatred and unfair judgment.

Hatred is one of Satan's oldest and greatest tricks. We believe we have the right to hate someone who has hurt us, and hesitant to forgive because we feel it is like letting them get away with it. However, in hating someone, we are letting them come between us and God. The Bible says that if we have hatred in our hearts, we are in darkness; and there can be no darkness in God. The Bible specifically warns us against it, yet millions of us fall prey to this trap of the enemy. Whether or not your hatred is related to race, you need to forgive and release it to God. Holding on to it won't make the situation any better. He's the only one who can heal your hurt.

"Judge not according to the appearance,
but judge righteous judgment."
–John 7:24

There are countless places in the Bible where we are warned about judging our fellow man. In fact, one passage says:

"Judge not, that ye be not judged."
–Matthew 7:1

We often want to make assumptions and quick judgments about people based on what we can see with our physical eyes. So much strife, hurt, and division could be avoided if we would stop judging one another. The Word says God looks on the heart, so let Him be the judge.

We've all seen the ugliness associated with racism. It can cause anguish, bitterness, rage, violence, and in some cases, even suicide. But racism always causes division. This isn't by accident. The enemy knows how dangerous the Body of Christ would be if it was completely united. Therefore, he has perverted the purpose of racial differences and caused it to be a dividing line when it should be a tool to strengthen and unify God's Kingdom on Earth.

Imagine for a moment a beautiful tapestry. If you look closely, you'll see threads of many different colors tightly interwoven to create the larger picture. Now, if you removed all the blue threads, part of the picture would be missing. Not only that, but the tapestry as a whole would be weaker and more prone to tearing. So it is with the Kingdom of God. Each culture brings their own flair to the picture, and without all the pieces, it's incomplete and weakened.

God loves variety. It's written in the very fabric of creation. He didn't create only one type of flower or one type of horse. Every species on Earth is varied, each beautiful in its own way. And though there are different species, they are interdependent. Even though flowers and bees are nothing alike, one cannot survive without the other, and we see this all throughout the Earth. So, if He created humans in the same manner, we should be looking at our differences as God intended, not as reasons for hatred and division.

When you are in a war, your skin color, social class, and culture don't matter to the soldier beside you. All that matters to him is that you are fighting on the same side. No matter what your physical or cultural differences, you all fight for the same purpose—to protect your family, freedom, and way of life. You are different, yet unified.

Like the soldiers, we too are engaged in warfare. Every day spiritual battles are being waged. No one soldier can win a war. It takes an entire army. Unity is a necessity of victory. The old saying, "United we stand, divided we fall," (Aesop, 1909) could not be more true. We need our brothers and sisters in Christ if we want to defeat our enemy. Yet, how many of our own fall to friendly fire? How can we possibly hope to gain victory over all the powers of Hell when we are so busy fighting among ourselves?

As we enter into the last days, we must guard against this tactic of the enemy. He will be fighting harder than ever to keep us divided, but we must band together as one body. Through unity we can help facilitate change in our nation.

God is the only answer to the crisis we now face, not just in our own nation, but in the world. The time for reformation has come, and it must begin in the church. Christians have been quiet far too long on this subject, afraid to speak out. We sit back and let it happen, not wanting to get involved because of the volatile nature of the issue. Instead, we huddle in our little corner of the world pointing fingers, laying blame at the feet of others, and using isolated Scripture to justify our actions.

Church, we have failed humanity. While we hide from our God-given responsibility to stand up for what is right, our enemy is prevailing.

Edmund Burke (1770) once said, "All that is necessary for the triumph of evil is that good men do nothing."

Look at the crisis our country is facing today. If the Church had been doing what it has been called to do, perhaps this could have all been avoided. It's time for the Church to rise up and challenge this spirit of racism. Stand up for the just and right cause, step forward, and be counted. Let the redeemed of the Lord say so! So, what do you say? Will you join me and answer this call to right the wrong?

CHAPTER 3

ORIGINS

I once saw a television interview with Dr. Billy Graham in which he was asked what problem he most desired to see eradicated in America. Without hesitation, Dr. Graham stated that he longed to see the racial division and strife in our nation overcome.

I wholeheartedly agree with his desire. It's been on my heart for many years now. However, I believe this change has to start with the church. We have to correct it in our own house before we can help heal our world. Without the body united as one, we'll never see the dissipation of racial tensions in our country. Race is a sensitive subject that needs to be approached and handled with a Godly perspective so we'll be able to move toward Biblical solutions and through that, bring about racial reconciliation.

My goal in writing this book is not to debate who's right or wrong or argue about who's been hurt most. The truth is, we all—people of every race—have been touched by racism in one way or another. It isn't just a problem specific to one or two races. We're all affected by this problem, and only through working together will we overcome it.

Now, in all fairness, great strides have been made in rectifying this problem in some facets of society. However, it still seems like we're trying to fight back the ocean, like we've barely scratched the surface. We continue to see violent acts pervading our society. No matter where we look or what part of the country we're in, we can still see racism like a stain on the land. Just like an ink stain on a white sheet, it refuses to wash out.

In order to remove this stain on society, we need to first get a Biblical perspective on race. Where did race originate?

It began with the Word of God. That is where we find the foundation of the problem and the location of the solution. There are many views and interpretations on the subject of race. I will attempt to showcase both the secular standpoint and the religious standpoint and show you the Biblical solution.

I'll start with the secular view. While many people believe racial distinctions didn't appear until after the people were scattered at the Tower of Babel, others subscribe to the environmental theory. This theory states that the differences in race can be explained by the evolution of a particular racial group due to their environment and geographical location.

For instance, according to this theory, Anglo-Saxons have lighter skin because of where they settled in Europe. The milder temperatures and distance from the equator were factors in the resulting skin tone. People who settled farther south, closer to the equator in countries such as Africa developed a much darker skin tone due to long-term exposure to extreme climates and harsher sunlight, while those in between, such as those in the Middle East developed a lighter, olive-toned skin color.

However, this is the secular standpoint—a theory of environment. Instead of a Biblical view, this is an evolutionary one which states that nature caused the different races, not God. This thinking directly contradicts the Scripture because it assumes that only fair-skinned people were created by God while other races came about by circumstance.

But Malachi 2:10 tells us:

> *"Have we not all one father? Hath not one God created us? Why do we deal treacherously every man against his brother, by profaning the covenant of our fathers?"*

God created all of us, no matter our race and He is no respecter of persons.

While those in secular society are content with this naturalistic explanation for racial origins, there are also those who seek to twist

Scripture to serve their own purposes. For instance, some people use the cursing of Ham in Genesis 9 to justify racial oppression. In America's early era of black slavery, this was a commonly taught doctrine within the churches. We've come a long way since those times, but there are still a few places where this false doctrine is still being taught.

If you aren't familiar with the story of Ham's curse, it can be found in Genesis chapter 9. The Scripture tells us that Noah, Ham's father, drank too much wine and passed out in his tent. Unfortunately, he was uncovered with his nakedness exposed. Ham passed by, and seeing his father's state went to get his brothers so they could laugh at their father. However, when Shem and Japheth arrived, they did the right thing and covered up Noah, going in backward so as not to dishonor their father by looking on his nakedness.

Because Ham did not do the right thing, his line of decedents was cursed. They would live in perpetual slavery. Some people use this story to try to give Biblical support to the slave trade and the idea that not all races are equal. They seek to validate the evils of racism by the backward teaching.

Those who believe this teach that Ham is the father of the African race; therefore, they were put on the earth to be servants, but it's not true. In fact, in Exodus 20:5 it says:

"Visiting the iniquity of the fathers upon the children unto the third and fourth generation of them that hate me."

The real truth is this, God:

"made of one blood all nations of men for to dwell on all the face of the earth."
—Acts 17:26

We have been genetically coded by God to be varied, just as any other species He created. He wrote this into His plan from the beginning of time. We may be varied, but we are all specially designed by God. Let's come together as His family in unity and change the way the world views race.

CHAPTER 4

THE EXCUSE OF HURT

History of Hurt

Let me ask you a question: When people do or say mean and hurtful things without provocation, what is your first thought? You automatically assume they're bad people, right? Believe it or not, that might not be true.

Have you ever stopped to consider that maybe they are also victims? Let's ponder the possibilities. Take, for instance, an animal with its foot caught in a trap. That animal is scared and in pain. At that moment, it knows nothing else. However, if anyone were to attempt to free the animal, it would try its best to bite them. Why is that? The animal is so consumed with its fear and pain it can't recognize help when it comes. People are no different.

I've often said that hurting people hurt people, and it is so true. Just like a wounded animal, those who are holding on to their pain will lash out at anyone nearby, regardless if they are trying to help them or just passing by. The truth is, you will never understand someone's pain unless you've lived their life. We need to make a genuine effort to understand and listen without judgment or criticism. If someone hurts me, I only see their actions, not the history behind those actions. It is tempting to react in anger. However, we must be careful not react in anger.

"Be not hasty in thy spirit to be angry: for anger resteth in the bosom of fools."

–Ecclesiastes 7:9

There is no wisdom in anger. It will do nothing to resolve the situation but will only serve to make it worse. Proverbs 29:22 says:

> *"An angry man stirreth up strife, and a furious*
> *man aboundeth in transgression."*

Letting anger take over your reaction pulls you into sin instead of bringing resolution. Violence is never the answer. We have to learn to recognize that those feelings are from the enemy. I realize that for most people, anger is a knee-jerk reaction when they are attacked. However, the closer you get to God and the more you operate in His love, the more you notice your reactions change. Instead of anger, compassion will be your reaction.

Compassion is the cure. We have to see past how people have treated us and identify with their underlying hurt. It could be anything: divorce, layoff, cancer, depression, fear, discrimination. Whatever the cause, we must display the same grace and mercy God has afforded to us. Only then can we stop the bleeding and begin to mend what has been broken. However, we must consciously decide to be compassionate. We can choose to either create a safe place for those who have been wounded, or we can cause a greater divide.

For those of you who are like a wounded animal, I have a message for you as well. You too have to give up this hurt. No matter how many times we hurt God, He always forgives us. Should we not also do the same for our fellow man? With God's help, it's possible to forgive and move past their trespasses against you. When you forgive, you not only bring peace to your own life but effect change in theirs as well.

But where do we start? How far back in this history of hurt do we go? You don't have to go back. Just start right where you are. Forgive all those who have caused you pain, hurt, humiliation, and hatred. Release that pain to God. Only then will you have that peace that passes all understanding and calm the storm raging inside of you. Proverbs 16:9 says:

> *"Man makes plans, but the Lord directs his steps."*

Let God handle it.

If we don't take a stand, our country will once again be reduced to the same division, fighting, and hatred it experienced during the Civil War of 1860s which led to Lincoln's assassination, and the race riots of the 1960s that led to the assassination of Dr. Martin Luther King, Jr. We cannot allow those kinds of setbacks to continue. Let's endeavor to turn criminal minds into Christian minds.

We observe several holidays faithfully every year, such as the National Day of Prayer proclaimed by presidents for May each year, in which we write a letter or place a call in an effort to reach out any way we can. So, I say we declare a National Day of Forgiveness. Reach out to those who have hurt you, or whom you have hurt. Let's start a healing campaign right now and end this history of hurt. Are you ready to let it begin with you?

Now You See Me

When captured by the tail, some geckos and other lizards will actually detach that part of the tail in order to escape. The detached section continues to wriggle and jerk so the predator believes it still has its prey, allowing the real lizard to slip away while the predator is distracted.

Satan very often uses a similar tactic, and the world is largely unaware of it. He uses people much like the lizard uses its tail. He creates a distraction so you don't see what's really going on. When people hurt you, do you ever stop to wonder if they're the *real* enemy? We automatically blame the person who has hurt us. It's an automatic reaction. However, they're only puppets and the puppeteer goes unnoticed.

Satan is constantly trying to derail your destiny. When you are at your weakest, he'll sneak into your life in whatever way he can. He'll put people in your life to try to distract you from the plan God has for your life. I know it's difficult to see, but the person who has hurt you is just as much a victim as you are. With this particular trick, Satan can essentially destroy two lives for the price of one. We forget what 2 Corinthians 12:9 tells us about God's power (that it is made perfect in our weakness), and we do not need to give the enemy a foothold to distract us because we can turn to God.

> *"He was a murderer from the beginning, and*
> *abode not in the truth, because there is no truth*
> *in him. When he speaketh a lie, he speaketh of his*
> *own: for he is a liar, and the father of it."*
>
> –John 8:44

Satan is the ultimate illusionist—the father of lies, according to the Bible. He's constantly trying to trick and mislead us. The lie we most often believe is that forgiveness is weakness. We believe that if we forgive someone, it's like letting them win somehow—that they've gotten away with their crime against us. Holding their offenses against them, in our eyes, is justice.

However, that couldn't be farther from the truth. The truth is that holding on to that pain and anger will only cause you hurt. No one is paying for your pain but you. Hate is a poison. It'll cause you to self-destruct if you don't let it go.

It's time we learn who our real enemy is.

It's not those who speak against us or lash out; the enemy is pulling the puppet strings behind the scenes. Instead of attacking our brothers and sisters, let's launch an attack on all of Hell. Too long Satan has stood in the shadows while others are punished for his crimes.

Let's endeavor to see past the person in front of us to the real enemy hiding beneath.

CHAPTER 5

PLACE OF PAIN

Pain is an individual affliction. The way it affects us is as unique as our fingerprints. Some of us have a low tolerance for pain and try to relieve it as soon as possible. Others, however, will endure a tremendous amount of pain before they seek relief. We believe it doesn't affect us, that it's functional pain.

The truth is, we've held on to it so long we've become comfortable with our pain.

I once heard a story of a dog who laid in the same spot in the corner of the porch every single day. Though the porch was spacious and the dog could have chosen any other spot to lay, he continued to return to the corner by the steps. This went on day after day, month after month, and year after year until the wood began to wear away. After a while, the dog began to notice that his side would hurt when he laid there. Time went on, and the pain became increasingly worse. Yet the dog continued to return to that spot, never thinking to lay somewhere else. Eventually, the pain became unbearable.

The dog's owner, realizing there was something wrong, went to investigate what was causing it. He soon discovered that as the dog wore away the wood, a nail had been exposed. It had dug into the dog's side day after day, tearing the skin to the point it had now become infected and required surgery. Sadly, it all could have been avoided had the dog moved to a different part of the porch when the pain began. Instead, he insisted on returning to his place of pain no matter how much it hurt him. In the end, it nearly cost him his life.

So many Christians are in the same situation as the dog. Many of us are "wounded warriors" who have become so accustomed to our situation that we are comfortable with our pain. No matter how much we try to cover it up and pretend it doesn't exist, it still affects us. We ignore the nails that wound us on a daily basis, failing to see the signs of the sickness it causes. Why do we do this? Because we believe our answer, our deliverance, or our miracle exists in that place. We've been there so long, we're afraid to leave.

So how do we break this habit? How do we regain control of our lives? Well, we certainly can't do it alone. In order to move on from our places of pain, we have to be willing to let it go. I know sometimes the pain has been with you so long it's sewn into the very fabric of your being. But trust me when I say that giving that pain over to God is the only way for you to move on with your life. Once you've relinquished your hold on your hurt, it's up to you to leave that place and never come back. Only *you* can move to a different spot on the porch. You will never completely heal if you don't. So many people these days talk about the change they would like to see, but they want to stay rooted to the same spot and are unwilling to get up and move.

Change doesn't find you by accident, nor does it come automatically. Change is a choice, a decision you have to make for yourself. No one else will do it for you. Become the very change you wish to see. It takes work, but it's worth it.

It's time we in the church leave our favorite place of pain and become trendsetters for peace.

"Well, Bishop you don't know how they've hurt me. It's their fault I'm this way."

No, no, no. Don't start playing the blame game.

"And why beholdest thou the mote that is in thy brother's eye, but considerest not the beam that is in thine own eye? Or how wilt thou say to thy brother, Let me pull out the mote out of thine eye; and, behold, a beam is in thine own eye? Thou hypocrite, first cast out the beam out of thine own eye; and then shalt thou see clearly to cast out the mote out of thy brother's eye."

–Matthew 7:3-5

It's your life. You can't be pointing your finger at someone else when the problem resides with you. You'll never be able to help this nation move past racism while you're carrying around all that hate and pain. Instead of focusing on how much you're hurting, let it go and move toward peace and healing.

It's time for a new spot on the porch!

CHAPTER 6

THE DANGER IN ANGER

A nger, as defined by Merriam-Webster, is *"a strong feeling of displeasure."* That displeasure can motivate us to do many things: hate, wound, ruin, humiliate, criticize, and destroy. Proverbs 22:24-25 says:

> *"Make no friendship with an angry man; and*
> *with a furious man thou shalt not go: Lest thou*
> *learn his ways, and get a snare to thy soul."*

Sometimes it's difficult for us to talk about our anger and explore the reasons behind it. We find it embarrassing or awkward to talk about. Admitting that we're angry or that we may have an anger problem can be uncomfortable. Maybe the cause of that anger is something deeply personal that we don't want anyone to know about. We make excuses for it like, "Well, I was just a little upset. That's why I acted that way," because it's easier to say than admitting we have a problem. True, people do get upset from time to time, but that still isn't admitting the problem; it's dancing around it. However, if you never admit to the problem, you can never be rid of it. You must expose it and deal with it. But how?

The Bible cautions us to be slow to anger. However, some people harbor anger like it's a heat-seeking missile. There's no warning or reasoning; they're just looking for a warm body to take out their anger on. That kind of anger is out of control and destructive. It can cause irreversible wounds and divides.

Ephesians 4:26 says:

"Be ye angry, and sin not: let not the sun go down upon your wrath: Neither give place to the devil."

Angry protestors who loot, burn buildings, and attack officers are examples of anger gone wrong. Too many people confuse the emotion of anger with how people react to it. Anger is an emotion.

God instilled in us the ability to be able to distinguish right from wrong. However, people tend to think of anger as bad and wrong because it's so often mismanaged. They associate rage, violence, and verbal beatings with anger, when anger isn't really the problem. How people react to it is the real culprit. In this case, the only things they accomplish are destruction, hurt, and causing more hatred. Proverbs 14:29 says it like this:

"Whoever is patient has great understanding, but one who is quick-tempered displays folly."

No problem was ever solved with rage and out of control behavior. It is not motivated by righteousness, but by revenge.

However, anger can also be used as motivation to effect changes and stop injustice. Righteous anger is not out of control, but rather, purposeful and productive. Our sense of right and wrong triggers this type of anger. It's a legitimate anger against injustice and wrongdoing. We see the mistreated and feel angry; we want to right the wrongs and defend those who cannot defend themselves. Righteous anger leads us to attack the problem, not the person.

This righteous anger turns ordinary people into heroes who shape the course of history. Anger at injustice led to our country's freedom, the abolishment of slavery, and gender equality laws, just to name a few. People like Abraham Lincoln and Dr. Martin Luther King Jr. knew how to use their anger for good instead of letting their anger use them.

Another prime example of routing your anger into something productive can be found in the story of Candace Lightner. In May, 1980,

Candace's thirteen-year-old daughter, Cari, was struck and killed by a drunk driver. The driver never even stopped. He just went on his way, leaving young Cari's body lying in the street like garbage.

Candace could have let her daughter's death fill her with bitterness and rage. However, she used her anger to affect change. Instead of letting her anger overcome her, she formed an organization called Mothers Against Drunk Drivers (MADD). Because of her efforts, laws have changed regarding drunk driving, and MADD has helped to raise awareness of this plight. That, my friend, is channeling anger into something productive.

The Bible holds many stories about anger—both righteous anger, and destructive anger. Genesis 4 tells the story of Cain and Abel. They had both prepared a sacrifice to God, but only Abel's offering was accepted because Cain gave it grudgingly. However, instead of being angry with himself and correcting his mistake, he chose violence. Cain attacked his brother and killed him out of rage. This is a prime example of out-of-control anger.

Anger left unchecked leads to devastation. I've felt instantaneous acute anger at times, and so have you. Everyone has. However, instead of focusing that energy on producing change, Satan wants us to focus it on destruction and chaos. Why? The Bible gives us the answer. In Proverbs 16:32, it says:

> "Better a patient person than a warrior, one
> with self-control than one who takes a city."

Not only is he afraid of what we could do, but we're doing his job for him. He doesn't have to try to destroy us; we're destroying ourselves.

We find in Numbers 20 where Moses' reaction to his anger cost him a great price. The Israelites were traveling through the desert and were desperate for water. They complained about Moses and murmured against him, and he was angry. However, God told him to speak to a rock in the place He had appointed, and water would flow. But Moses, still angry with the people, didn't obey God. Instead, he struck the rock in order to make a spectacle and prove a point. Unfortunately, Moses let his anger get the best of him. Because of his mistake, he was not allowed into the Promised Land.

You may recall in 2 Samuel where the prophet Nathan was sent by God to give King David a message. Nathan told David of a rich man who owned a multitude of flocks. However, when the rich man had a guest and needed to feed him, he stole a sheep from his neighbor, a poor man. David was enraged at the injustice. He declared that the rich man should be put to death for his crimes.

Then Nathan said, *Thou art the man.* He pointed out that David had many, many wives and all the riches he could ever hope for. And yet, he sent Uriah the Hittite out to battle where he was sure to die. Why? Because he wanted Uriah's wife for his own. Nathan pointed out his double-mindedness to David, and he had to lay down his pride and face his own sin. He used his anger to create change in his own life.

Another example of anger can be found in the life of Jesus. In this example, we see what *righteous* anger looks like. Matthew 21 tells the story of Jesus entering the temple and finding people treating the temple as a place of commerce instead of a holy place. A righteous anger rose up within him, and he put right that which was wrong.

> *"Then Jesus went into the temple of God and drove out all those who bought and sold in the temple, and overturned the tables of the money changers and the seats of those who sold doves. And He said to them, "It is written, 'My house shall be called a house of prayer, but you have made it a 'den of thieves.'"*
>
> –Matthew 21:12-13

Again in Mark 3:5 we see where Jesus' anger was aroused. A man with a withered hand was in the synagogue one day. Jesus, of course, healed the man, but the Pharisees frowned on it and accused Jesus of wrongdoing. The Bible says:

> *"He {Jesus} looked around at them in anger and, {was} deeply distressed at their stubborn hearts..."*

Jesus was angered by the injustice of the Pharisees. It's okay to feel anger. It does not, however, give you license to destroy.

Anger can be dealt with in two different ways. Repression and expression. Repression is when you bottle up all that anger inside you and refuse to acknowledge it. It is dangerous and unhealthy. Not only can repressed anger be mentally and spiritually draining, but it can even start to manifest physically in your body. It's not what you're eating that is making you sick, but what's eating you. Studies link repressed anger with a myriad of diseases such as cancer and heart irregularities. If you keep all that anger pent up inside you, it will eventually destroy you. You have to let it go.

Which brings me to the other way anger can be dealt with—expression. Expression can be bad or good, depending on how you convey your anger. Too many associate expression with aggression, but they're not the same thing. It's okay to be angry because of injustice, but violence and hatred are not the answer. Instead, take the negative feelings and do something positive with them. In doing so, you can begin to solve problems instead of adding to them.

CHAPTER 7

BRIDGING THE GAP

I was once told a story about a visitor to a mental hospital for the criminally insane. Upon arriving at the hospital, the visitor was shocked to see only three guards supervising about four hundred inmates. That was over one hundred inmates to one guard. Disturbed, the visitor approached one of the guards and asked if he ever worried about the prisoners planning and executing an escape. The guard smiled and shook his head, saying he wasn't worried at all because the insane never unite.

Never before have I seen such hatred among the brethren as I do nowadays. Every time I turn around I'm hearing news of unrest. The last days are drawing closer, and the enemy will be fighting all the harder.

Now, more than ever, we need to come together as a unified body. It's insanity to think we can go to war against all the powers of darkness without our kindred. The word kindred doesn't just mean blood relatives; in the Church it means people joined together by God's grace. Think of it this way: grace, g-race, God's Race. When Jesus died on the cross, we all were grafted into His lineage, His bloodline. We are no longer a separated people. We are all a part of the Body of Christ, brothers and sisters through Him. We may have come over in different boats, but we're in the same boat now.

Take, for example, the United States Olympic Team. It's comprised of people from all different racial backgrounds, all different cultures. However, when someone from the U. S. team wins, it's our national anthem that plays, not a song to reflect the individual's personality. Why is that? Because regardless of skin color or culture, he or she is still an American.

Shouldn't it be the same with the Church? We may look different or come from different backgrounds, but we're all children of God.

So how do we pull together? How do we bridge that gap? First, we must get a Biblical perspective on the matter because without God, this is an impossible task.

Isaiah 66:18 shows where God says:

> *"I will gather all nations and tongues; and*
> *they shall come, and see My glory."*

Did you see that? He will gather *all* nations and tongues. Not only some. When God created the different races, He intended for our cultures to complement one another. Think of the different cultures like an orchestra. Each instrument is beautiful in its own right, creating a sound that no other instrument can. However, when many different instruments play together in harmony, it creates a beautiful melody that could never be accomplished by any one instrument. Such is the Body of Christ. The Bible says in Psalm 139 that we are *fearfully and wonderfully made.* Each culture is unique and beautiful; each brings a part of the melody.

> *"For by one Spirit are we all baptized into one body,*
> *whether we be Jews or Gentiles, whether we be bond*
> *or free; and have all been made to drink into one*
> *Spirit. For the body is not one member, but many."*
>
> –1 Corinthians 12:13-14

God created us to be different, crafting each person according to the role we have to play in the Body of Christ. He instilled in each of us talents and gifts that are uniquely ours and specific to our task. The Bible goes on to say in verse 18:

> *"God set the members every one of them in*
> *the body, as it hath pleased Him."*

I can't do what God has called you to do any more than a nose can hear. Likewise, God doesn't need you to be exactly like me. He needs you to fulfill the task He specifically designed you to accomplish.

Instead of letting our racial distinctions become a barrier between us, we should be celebrating our differences. After all, God gave us distinctive backgrounds and cultures for a reason. He designed our races to operate smoothly and in conjunction with one another without losing our cultural distinctions. Too often we simply tolerate one another. In doing so, we miss the rich culture and diversity our brothers and sisters bring to the body. We all have our parts to play in the kingdom, but without unity we cannot accomplish that which God has planned for us.

Now that we see things from a Biblical standpoint, it's time to look inward. Before we can begin to build a bridge between the races, we must first examine ourselves. Racism can be a sneaky sin, and it can take many forms. It can be either seen—as in cases where violence and verbal abuse are present; or unseen—where the sin occurs in the heart and mind without any outward sign. As Christians, we must constantly examine ourselves, checking our thoughts and actions against the Word of God so we don't fall prey to this trap.

1 Corinthians 13:5 says it like this:

> *"Examine and test and evaluate your*
> *own selves to see whether you are holding to your faith*
> *and showing the proper fruits of it. Test and prove yourselves.*
> *Do you not yourselves realize and know thoroughly by an*
> *ever-increasing experience that Jesus Christ is in you—unless*
> *you are counterfeits disapproved on trial and rejected."*

Maybe you've never been mean or degrading to a person of another race but have judged them in your mind. Or perhaps you hate those whose race is different from your own, though you never speak your hatred aloud. Whether or not there is physical manifestation, it's still sin. The Bible tells us in 1 Samuel 16:7:

"For the Lord seeth not as man seeth; for man looketh on the outward appearance, but the Lord looketh on the heart."

When you're aligned with Him, you'll begin to see a shift, not only in your own life, but in the lives of those you come into contact with. His love is the bridge that spans the distance between races, and brings us together.

CHAPTER 8

THE POWER OF BROTHERHOOD

Unity Breeds Harmony

Racism has never been about color, it's about division. For generations Satan has worked to keep us divided, and racism has been one of his greatest tools. From the persecution of the Jews to slavery to the issues we face in modern America, Satan is constantly fighting to maintain this divide. Not only through racism either. Division comes in many forms: male and female, old and young, wealthy and poor. There's even division among church denominations. Have you ever stopped to wonder why? Because the prospect of a unified body scares the devil. What would happen if the Church would stand united, embracing our cultural differences? Hell wouldn't stand a chance, and Satan would have a good reason to be concerned.

Now, more than ever, there is a need to keep unity among the brethren. The only way to produce unity is by allowing the Holy Spirit to work through us and the love of God to guide us. It's not something you can manufacture. Only with God is it possible. Granted, it's not always easy. It's something that will take hard work and effort on our parts. You have to be willing to fully invest in it and constantly maintain it. This isn't just a one-time meal or occasional fellowship meeting. It's time for us to put aside our own agendas and feelings and put forth genuine effort.

Paul said it like this in 1 Corinthians 1:10:

*"Now I beseech you, brethren, by the name of our Lord
Jesus Christ, that ye all speak the same thing, and that there
be no divisions among you; but that ye be perfectly joined
together in the same mind and in the same judgment."*

Unity, as defined by Dictionary.com, is the state of being combined
into one, as the parts of a whole. The Bible calls it being of one mind and
one accord. Unity is a divine calling for the Body of Christ. We are one
in Him. It's what we were made for. However, many confuse unity with
uniformity. Unity is not sameness; it's being of one purpose. We were not
created to be cookie-cutter Christians.

The beautiful thing about the Church is that where one person is
weak another will be strong and vice versa. Our diversities complement
one another, so when we work together in unity we are complete. There
can be such diversity in our gifts and yet we are still of one spirit. That
is the principle with which God designed us. He made the different
cultures to work together in harmony. So as brothers and sisters in
Christ, we can be unified in our efforts. We're on the same team, fighting
for the same cause.

Psalm 133:1 says:

*"Behold how good and how pleasant it is for
brethren to dwell together in unity."*

And where there is unity, there will also be harmony. It doesn't
matter if you're a judge or a janitor, rich or poor, a lawyer or a laborer.
This is a bicycle built for two, so jump on and let's do this together! We
are the family of God.

Let's look at an analogy of a basketball team. The coach evaluates all
player and places them where they are the strongest. If all the players had
the same talents and were strong in the same area, the team would never
win a game. They would be destined for failure. However, if you have
five different players with strengths in different areas, then you have a

real chance. Their differences make them stronger and make them a formidable opponent. It's time we, as a body, realize that our differences make us a stronger team.

There are those, however, who love to sow dissension among the ranks. Instead of embracing difference, they try to magnify it, driving a wedge between people. They are constantly trying to reopen old wounds or create new divides. Beware that you don't give in to these tricks. The enemy will put people in your life specifically to get you off track and break up any chance at unity. Paul warned against this in Romans 16:17-18.

> *"Now I beseech you, brethren, mark them which cause divisions and offences contrary to the doctrine which ye have learned; and avoid them. For they that are such serve not our Lord Jesus Christ, but their own belly; and by good words and fair speeches deceive the hearts of the simple."*

It's impossible for the world to find and keep peace without the Prince of Peace. However, how can we introduce the world to the love of Christ when we don't have it in our own lives? We have to live that love or others will never see it or listen to our message. With so much hatred and fighting among us, it's no wonder the world wants nothing to do with Christianity. It's time we pull together and take this world by storm. The enemy won't know what hit him!

Going forward, instead of seeing our differences as a dividing line, see them for what they were meant to be—the tools that bring us together. The walls of division must be broken down: walls between races, walls between the sexes, walls between denominations, and walls between social classes. Let's come together as one body united against the enemy. Let's take back our nation, and bring an end to this violence and hatred. It's time we learn to appreciate, celebrate, and embrace our differences, whether they are racial, social, or gender-based.

Bond of Peace

The word *bond* comes from the Greek *sundesmo* which means to closely identify with or to have a union which produces harmony between members joined closely together. We are bound together through Christ with his love as a bonding agent—spiritual glue that holds us together. Colossians 2:19 says it like this:

> *"And not holding the Head, from which all the body by joints and bands having nourishment ministered, and knit together, increaseth with the increase of God."*

Just as a physical body is comprised of many different parts, such as ligaments, joints, and bones, so too is the Body of Christ. Without all of those parts working in unity, the entire body suffers. We were made for togetherness and fellowship, not for separation and alienation. We need our fellow humans. Only by working together to fulfill our calling can we bring peace to our nation. There should be no dissent or debate; no separation or fragmentation; no black church or white church; no us and them. There is simply one body, together, united under God.

The word *one* doesn't always have to mean singular or alone; it can be a collection of diverse things. Many cities make up a state, many apartments make up one unit, and many members make up the Body of Christ. As the body, we are to promote unity and peace, not destroy it.

What is peace? Peace, according to dictionaryfocus.com, is a state of tranquility, quiet, and harmony free from civil disturbance, war, and oppressive or unpleasant thoughts and emotions. Peace is what our country needs. But without Jesus there is no peace. We, as the Church, are called to walk in peace instead of turmoil, rioting, and protest. We should have peace with one another because we have the Prince of Peace within.

We are God's representatives. As such, we cannot allow racism and discrimination into our lives. Don't judge someone based on their social status, gender, race, or culture. To do so goes against God. It's contrary to the Bible, immoral, evil, and unchristian (not Christian it is because not Christ-like). How can we promote unity if we are disjointed?

Many have tried to find Biblical justifications for their wrongdoing, using isolated Scriptures to legitimize their obsession with separation and discrimination. They use stories like the Tower of Babel where God declared that human beings would be separate, scattered, and unable to communicate, and He confused their languages. However, that was not the intention for mankind. It was because they were working together against God that He separated them. We know this was not God's plan for His children. In Acts 2:5-6, the Scripture tells us that God reversed the inability to communicate when at Pentecost, the Holy Spirit gave disciples the ability to speak in tongues and people from all nationalities heard the Good News in their own language.

> *"Seeing that ye have put off the old man with his deeds; And have put on the new man, which is renewed in knowledge after the image of Him that created him: Where there is neither Greek nor Jew, circumcision nor uncircumcision, Barbarian, Scythian, bond, nor free: but Christ is all and in all."*
>
> –Colossians 3:9-11

When the church was birthed into existence, it was a fellowship—a family that banded together to care for and protect one another.

Eventually, when the church spread to Greece, it became more of a philosophy.

Rome institutionalized it.

Europe developed it into a culture.

When Christianity crossed the ocean to America, we saw it as a way to make money and converted it into an enterprise. Through the generations and conversions, we've lost what it really means to be a part of the church.

We need to get back to the roots of fellowship that were present in the beginning. The body needs that sense of family and support once more. In Ephesians 4:5-6, Paul said that we are one body, with one Lord and one faith.

Let's get back to what we were meant for—fellowship and family. It's time we come together, united in the bond of peace and begin to spread love and healing throughout our nation.

It Takes Two

In previous chapters, I touched on the subject of kinship in the church, but I wanted to get a little deeper into it. I truly believe this lesson is vital to the Body of Christ. The whole point of this current upheaval—the enemy's master plan behind the issue of racism—is division. If Satan is fighting so hard to keep us apart, don't you think that's a good reason to come together?

The Bible talks often about unity and the importance of fellowship and brotherhood. Why would it be mentioned so many times? Because it's important. Together we are more powerful, more profitable, more productive, and more protected.

I see three main points the Bible discusses regarding unity. The first is that we were designed to be reliant on one another. It's woven into our souls. We *need* one another—probably more than we realize. One tree alone cannot withstand the wind. One player cannot win against a whole team. One brick never made a beautiful structure. The Lone Ranger had Tonto. Batman had Robin. We need one another.

> *"Two are better than one; because they have a good reward for their labour. For if they fall, the one will lift up his fellow: but woe to him that is alone when he falleth; for he hath not another to help him up. Again, if two lie together, then they have heat: but how can one be warm alone? And if one prevail against him, two shall withstand him; and a threefold cord is not quickly broken."*
> –Ecclesiastes 4:9-12

We are supposed to be there for one another in good times and in bad. If you fall down, I will help you back up. If you get lost along the way, I'll come looking for you. If you're hurt, I'll be there to help you heal. That is how the Church is supposed to be. You shouldn't ever have to be alone.

The Bible says in Psalm 133:

"Behold, how good and how pleasant it is for
brethren to dwell together in unity!"

Did you see that? Brethren. Not Blacks, Whites, Hispanics, or any other nationality—brethren. Sometimes we tend to put our culture before our Creator. We define ourselves by our culture before we define ourselves by our God. We identify ourselves first as white or black when we should be first and foremost Christians.

If we were to accept our heritage as Christians, the lines between our cultures would dissolve. The truth is, since Christ's great work on the cross, we are all of one heritage—joint heirs with Christ.

Do you remember what it was like on September 11, 2001? Do you remember watching the towers fall? That day we weren't separated by culture. We all mourned together. Not as White, Black, Asian, or Hispanic, but as Americans. If we can come together like that in tragedy, why can we not come together in victory?

The Bible says in Acts 17 that God:

"hath made of one blood all nations of men
for to dwell on all the face of the earth."

We are all of the same culture now. Let's embrace that.

The second point the Bible makes is that when we come together, things happen that couldn't ordinarily happen. With our fellow Christians, we can overcome great obstacles and affect great change. Matthew 18:19-20 says:

"Again I say unto you, that if two of you shall agree
on earth as touching any thing that they shall ask,
it shall be done for them of my Father which is in
heaven. For where two or three are gathered together
in my name, there am I in the midst of them."

Unity among the brethren will always invite the Holy Spirit in. It grabs His attention, and pulls Him into action.

> *"And five of you shall chase an hundred, and a hundred of you shall put ten thousand to flight: and your enemies shall fall before you by the sword."*
>
> –Leviticus 26:8

The simple, Biblical truth is that together we are far greater than when alone. God designed it that way. That's why a united Church has the enemy trembling in fear. He knows he wouldn't stand a chance against us. If we were to be truly united, we could take back all that the enemy has stolen from us and all we've allowed him to cheat us out of. We're coming into the last days. The time for us to come together is now.

> *"Can two walk together, except they be agreed?"*
>
> –Amos 3:3

The third point the Bible makes is that we cannot accomplish any of this if we continue to accentuate our differences. In order for us to truly unite, we have to let those differences go and instead focus on our similarities. Don't misunderstand, I'm not saying we have to give up our culture or heritage. I'm only saying that we need to see how alike we all are in our kinship through Christ.

If we can put aside our own feelings and agendas and get the mind and heart of Christ, we can change the fate of not only this nation but of our entire world. It's time we go on the offensive and take back what has been stolen. Let's show Satan that he has a good reason to be afraid. Reform starts here.

CHAPTER 9

A PURE HEART

Consistent In Character

I've been the victim of racial discrimination on many occasions, and I know firsthand how deeply it hurts to be judged by the color of your skin. I've never experienced anything more degrading or humiliating. At times it seems impossible not to react defensively when someone mistreats you. However, I learned early on that no matter how deeply someone hurts you, you cannot let their actions affect your character. Consistency is powerful. When you become so in tune with God that you don't let people change who you are in Him, you'll find peace and strength like you've never known.

Strength of character is a mark of maturity. All great men in the Bible had this in common—Joseph, David, Job, and Jesus, to name a few. Even in times of great adversity, they were steadfast in their faith and let God guide their actions.

This is most apparent in the life of Jesus. The issues faced as a victim of racism are extraordinarily similar to those Jesus faced in His own life. The Bible says in Hebrews 4:15:

> *"For we have not a high priest which cannot be touched with the feeling of our infirmities; but was in all points tempted like as we are, yet without sin."*

In Jesus' time, the land was occupied by Rome, a nation which considered Jews to be filth, and Romans persecuted them mercilessly.

Not only that, but Jesus was also hated by people of His own race. The people He grew up with rejected and mocked Him. Everywhere He went, He was met with hatred, confrontation, and even violence. Yet in all this, He never once reacted with anger; never once did He try to hurt those who had hurt Him; never once did His character falter. Instead, He exuded love and displayed mercy.

How did He accomplish all of that? We see the answer in John 12: 49:

> *"For I have not spoken of myself; but the Father*
> *which sent me, he gave me a commandment,*
> *what I should say, and what I should speak."*

Jesus only reacted with love, and only spoke what the Father told Him. He let God guide Him by aligning His character with God's character. Imagine what would happen if more of us lived our lives that way. What would happen if we only spoke from the heart of God? Well, the world would be a lot different.

Another prime example of character can be found in the life of Joseph. He was betrayed by his own brothers. They threw him into a pit, then sold him to passing slavers. He spent the next several years of his life in slavery and a good deal of time in prison, all because of what his brothers had done.

If anyone ever had a reason to be bitter or to hate those who had hurt them, it was Joseph. However, a time came when Joseph had the opportunity to either save his family or let them starve. Their lives were literally in his hands. He could have easily let their actions affect his decision or let his own hurt rule the situation, but he didn't. True to his character, Joseph let the love of God guide him. As a result, he not only saved his family, but restored his relationship with them and brought peace to the situation.

They say if you spend an abundance of time with someone, you start to take on some of their characteristics. The same can be said of your relationship with God. As you grow closer to God, your character begins to mesh with His. When you reach that place, who you are in God becomes unshakeable. No matter what hurt you experience, no matter how people treat you, you remain steadfast. It doesn't matter what storms come your way, you have the peace of God.

The chain of racial hurt has been never-ending. The dominoes just keep falling, taking down one person after another. You've hurt me, so I'm going to hurt you back. Where will it end if not with you? Don't let someone else's actions guide yours. Have the courage and the strength of character to stand for what is right, no matter the cost. It's going to take strong men and women of God to effectively make a change in this nation.

Let's look at Dr. Martin Luther King Jr. for a moment. History will forever remember him as a leader in the African-American Civil Rights Movement. Because of his efforts, our nation was forever changed. Have you ever wondered why he was so wildly successful? The answer is simple. Because of his strength of character. No matter what kind of adversity he faced, Dr. King was devoted to the idea of nonviolence. Although he faced many things in his life (verbal abuse, physical violence, and police brutality), he never gave in, never reacted violently.

Repaying hate with more hate is just playing into Satan's plan. Now instead of one person sinning, it becomes two, and so on and so forth.

1 John 5:18 says:

"We know that whosoever is born of God sinneth not; but he that is begotten of God keepeth himself, and that wicked one toucheth him not."

We need to get to that place. A place where we don't allow the action of others to pull us away from God and His plans for us. Instead of letting adversity destroy our character, let it instead define our character.

Violence to Victory

I want to briefly look at the life of Joseph. He was sold into slavery by his own brothers, thrown into a pit, and went to prison for something he didn't do. In short, he had a rough go of it. Joseph could've let his hardships change his character or cause him to be bitter and unloving;

yet, despite all the he went through because of his brothers' treachery, he was still able to not only forgive them, but save their lives as well.

Because of Joseph's compassion and forgiveness, restoration and reconciliation occurred, instead of retaliation. By letting God guide his actions, Joseph brought his family from violence to victory.

With so many voices crying out for violence it's easy to see why there is upheaval these days. But where are the voices of victory? Why has the Church been so quiet on the issue of racism when we should be vocal and visible? We should be leading the way to reconciliation. Yet so many in the body turn a blind eye to this issue, afraid to address it or cause ripples.

Too many of us are so busy trying to be politically correct that we forget about being Biblically correct. Too many are worried about keeping people happy instead of staying in line with God's Word. It's time we stop caring how others perceive us and concern ourselves with staying in the will of God.

Thanks to all the media coverage of recent events, what's wrong with the world is exposed on a daily basis. Christ too saw the problems, but instead of adding to the problem, He fought and ultimately died to bring a solution. Jesus reached out to those who had been rejected and were despised, scorned, and excluded. He dined with evildoers and those considered to be unworthy.

The Pharisees were offended by Jesus' behavior, and criticized him for it, asking why he would eat with sinners and tax collectors, to which He replied that those who are well do not need a physician.

The world needs more people like Joseph—people who understand that the only way we should be repaying wrongdoing is with forgiveness. If someone hurts you and you react by hurting them back, where will it end?

Violence begets violence. But when you forgive, that cycle is broken and restoration can begin. Believe me, I know it's not easy. However, God commands us to forgive. If we hold on to that offense instead of letting it go, we are just as much in sin as the one who hurt us.

In Matthew 18:23-34 Jesus tells the story of a servant who owed a great debt to his king. When he couldn't pay, the king ordered that he be sold along with his wife, children, and everything he possessed. But the man begged the king to have mercy and said if the king would just be patient he would pay back everything he owed. The king was moved with compassion, and he released him, forgave him, and canceled all of his debt.

However, that same servant was owed money by another man, and he wasn't as kind to the man as the king had been to him. Instead, he took the man by the throat and demanded payment.

When the king found out, he became angry and scolded the servant for not having compassion on the man who owed him money. In his wrath, the king delivered the servant to the torturers until his debt had been paid.

Matthew 35 goes on to say:

> *"So also My heavenly Father will deal with every one of you if you do not freely forgive your brother from your heart his offenses."* AMP

Forgiveness is something God takes very seriously. The Bible tells us if we want our sins to be forgiven, we must also forgive those who have hurt us. Don't let your hurt come between you and God. Let it go and forgive. It's not easy, but I think you'll find that once you have forgiven someone, it not only changes his or her life, but yours as well. Just like we have a National Day of Prayer, let's begin a National Day of Forgiveness.

Plea for Pardon

Our nation is in a state of great social turmoil. Greed, selfishness, and prejudices are tearing us apart at the seams. Every time I turn on my television, the news is reporting on a new act of violence. It seems as though there will be no end to the bloodshed, no solution to this problem.

But cheer up, because I've come to tell you that there is a solution—forgiveness. Forgiveness is the answer for all of your hurts: past, present, and future. And it's available to anyone who will acknowledge, confess, repent, and forsake their evil ways.

God wants to take us back to the basics of forgiveness. It's time we as a nation relearn what it means to forgive. Forgiveness is so much more than ignoring or forgetting an offense. To forgive is to no longer hold it against the offender and make an effort to restore the broken relationship. Whether or not you forget it, you cannot carry a grudge. Why?

Matthew 6:15 says:

> *"But if ye forgive not men their trespasses,*
> *neither will your Father forgive you."*

We must forgive those who have sinned against us if we are going to experience the forgiveness of God.

Despite the fact that people try to ignore, deny, excuse, or conceal sin, the reality of it remains painfully present. You can't just sweep it under the rug or hide it in a closet. Whether or not you acknowledge it, it continues to affect both you and those around you until it's dealt with. Sin sears the conscience, creating a divide, not just between you and others, but between you and the Father as well.

Forgiveness isn't only for the benefit of the offender. If you have an unforgiving spirit, you are cut off from God. Offense blocks the channels by which you have peace and happiness. Without that connection to the Father, your spirit will wither and die as a fruit removed from the vine.

Furthermore, holding on to offense can have a dire effect on your physical body. Scientists have concluded that people who suppress toxic negative emotions such as anger, hatred, resentment, and grief are far more likely to develop cancer than others. Other illnesses such as heart disease and stroke have also been linked to unforgiveness. By refusing to forgive, we are literally killing ourselves.

It's no wonder the Bible says:

> *"The thief cometh not, but for to steal,*
> *and to kill, and to destroy. . ."*
>
> –John 10:10

The devil uses whatever sins he can to effectively reach his goal. Unforgiveness is one of his favorite and most effective tools.

But how many times can we be expected to forgive someone? There has to be a limit, right? Wrong.

We find in Matthew 18 where Peter comes to Jesus, asking him exactly that. Verse 21 says:

"Then came Peter to him, and said, Lord, how oft shall my brother sin against me, and I forgive him? Till seven times?"

Sometimes it can be very difficult to forgive those who have hurt us, especially when they have sinned against us repeatedly. However, look at what Jesus says to Peter in verse 22:

"Jesus saith unto him, I say not unto thee, until seven times: but until seventy times seven."

No matter how many times, or how badly you've been hurt, you must forgive. It's our duty as Christians to follow God's direction on this, regardless of our personal feelings.

There are countless times in the Bible where we are commanded to forgive those who have wronged us. Matthew 5:39 says:

"Whosoever shall smite thee on thy right cheek, turn to him the other also."

Instead of fighting back or retaliating, we're commanded to turn the other cheek.

We see this in 1 Samuel 24. King Saul is hunting David, intending to kill him. While seeking him, Saul went into a cave to relieve himself. Little did he know that David and his men were hiding in that same cave watching him. David could have easily killed him. In fact, his men encouraged him to do just that. But David refused, despite the fact this was the twentieth time Saul had tried to kill him. Had it been the other way around, Saul would've killed David without a second thought. Instead, David snuck up and cut off the hem of Saul's robe to prove that he could have killed him but didn't. Because David refused to retaliate and kept his heart right, God promoted him, and he became King of Israel.

When David finally confronted Saul in verse 12, he said:

> *"May the Lord judge between me and you,*
> *and may the Lord avenge me upon you, but*
> *my hand shall not be upon you."* AMP

We have to remember that seeking revenge and trying to get even with others is not our right. God says:

> *"Vengeance is mine, and I will repay."*
> –Romans 12:19

We've been charged by God to forgive and bring restoration to the people. It's time for the Church to own up to this unmet obligation to God, others, and ourselves. We have to purge our hearts of malice, envy, hatred, and a desire for revenge if we truly want to see change. It's time we answer this plea for pardon.

CHAPTER 10

A PRAYER FOR THE NATION

O   ur leaders have the power to forever change the course of our nation. When things go wrong, however, it's easier to blame those in power than to try to become part of the solution. But blaming them does nothing to change the situation. Prayer does. I know it's sometimes difficult to support our leaders, and you don't have to agree with them, but the Bible does say you have to pray for them.

Whether or not we agree on political issues, I think we can all agree that we need to pray for wisdom where our government is concerned. The choices our leaders make will affect generations to come, not just concerning the issue of race, but in all of their decisions. If we had spent as much time praying for them as we have spent tearing them down, our nation might not have reached this state of crisis.

"First of all, then, I urge that supplications, prayers, intercessions, and thanksgivings be made for all people, for kings and all who are in high positions, that we may lead a peaceful and quiet life, godly and dignified in every way. This is good, and it is pleasing in the sight of God our Savior."

–Timothy 2:1-2

Paul encouraged Timothy in his letter to pray for those in power that they may have peace in the land. Not only that, but he goes on to say that it pleases God when we pray for them. Now, it's important to realize who was in power at the time that Paul wrote that letter. The ruler of Rome in that time was Nero Claudius Caesar Augustus Germanicus.

Nero was one of the most corrupt men who ever lived. Not only did he have elicit relationships, but he held public orgies as well. Nero was probably best known for persecuting Christians. Records have been found that tell of him capturing Christians, dipping them in oil, and setting them on fire as a source of light for his garden at night, along with all manner of other gruesome torture. Yet Paul told Timothy to pray for all those in authority.

> *"As it is written you shall not speak*
> *evil of a ruler of your people."*
> —Acts 23:5

If you can't bring yourself to pray for your leaders, at least stop talking bad about them. The Bible tells us life and death are in the power of the tongue. As a Christian, your words are endued with power, whether for good or for evil, so stop speaking negative things over our leaders today; instead speak wisdom and understanding.

King Saul tried multiple times to kill David, but David knew better than to come against him because Saul was the one God had set as ruler. There are many examples of God's wrath toward someone who'd spoken out against their leaders. It's a dangerous game to play, so I encourage you to pray for them instead. The fate of our country depends on men and women of God keeping our leaders lifted up.

CHAPTER 11

MUTED MOUTHS

In the Old Testament, watchmen were posted along the walls of the cities. Their jobs were to keep an eye out for any approaching danger and to sound the alarm should danger arise. At the first sign of trouble, the watchman would sound a trumpet so the people in the city were prepared to ward off the enemy when they arrived at the gates.

Where are our watchmen today? Christian leaders, *you* are the watchmen. We have been silently watching the enemy, letting him take over our land. It's time we open our mouths, and warn the people!

> *"But if the watchman see the sword come, and blow not the trumpet, and the people be not warned; if the sword come, and take any person from among them, he is taken away in his iniquity; but his blood will I require at the watchman's hand."*
>
> –Ezekiel 33:6

As leaders in the church, our God-appointed job is to warn the people of danger. With that job also comes a warning. If you fail to sound the alarm, the blood of the people will be on your hands. However, if you do warn them and they still won't listen, your hands are clean. You've done your job; the rest is up to them.

> *"His watchmen are blind: they are all ignorant, they are all dumb dogs, they cannot bark; sleeping, lying down, loving to slumber."*
>
> –Isaiah 56:10

I believe there are too many silent leaders today. Isaiah called them dumb dogs that can't bark. Or in some cases, won't bark. As leaders, we are essentially the guard dogs of the Church. Our bark is meant to alert the Church to danger or run a thief out of our neighborhood. We are there to expose the evil before it can take root and grow.

I've been waiting to hear our Christian leaders speak up and take a stand against this divide in our country but have been disappointed when all I hear is silence from them. How can we, as leaders, stand by quietly while this spirit of racism is tearing our country apart? We've stepped back and let politics take over. However, it's not a political issue, it's a spiritual one. We've been given a mandate from God to cry aloud and lift up our voices like a trumpet in Zion! Speak up and speak out. Someone, somewhere, please stand up and say something! Stop the violence, unite as one, forgive one another, and walk in the love of God.

CHAPTER 12

WILLFUL BLINDNESS

In Luke chapter 10, Jesus preached to a crowd that had gathered. The Bible tells us that during his sermon, a man stood up and asked what he had to do to inherit eternal life.

Jesus asked him what was written in the law.

The man replied, saying that according to the law he must love God with all of his heart, soul, strength, and mind, and that he must love his neighbor as he loved himself. If the man did as He had said, he would have eternal life. However, the man was determined to acquit himself of reproach, and went on to ask who, exactly, his neighbor was.

Jesus then told what has become perhaps one of the best-known stories in the Bible. He spoke of a man who was traveling on the road from Jerusalem to Jericho. Along the way, the man was attacked by a band of robbers. He was beaten nearly to death, robbed of his clothes and all his belongings, and left in the ditch to die.

A priest traveling along the same road happened upon the man. However, the priest chose to ignore him and passed by on the other side of the road.

The same thing happened when a Levite chanced upon the man; he passed by without bothering to help.

Finally, a passing Samaritan came upon the man. Unlike the two before him, the Samaritan was moved with compassion toward the man. Instead of passing on by, the Samaritan went to him and cleaned and bound his wounds. When he had finished, he helped the man up onto his own donkey, and took him to an inn where he paid for his care. An important thing to note is that the man's culture treated Samaritans as second-class citizens and refused to talk to them, so this Samaritan's actions were even more impressive because of his attitude.

When Jesus finished the story, he commanded that we do likewise. However, we as the Church have fallen short of that mark. The body, as a whole, is reluctant to become involved in this issue. True, while many of us are not racists, we've refused to help those who are most in need. We tend to ignore things because they are socially acceptable, though morally wrong. Or we view racism as a social or legal problem.

But racism isn't a problem for the world to solve. It's a spiritual problem—a sin—and should be dealt with as such. However, instead of getting our hands dirty or expending any effort, we chose to ignore the pain outside of our own front door. We pass by on the other side of the road just like the Priest and the Levite. Maybe race has no real effect on your life, but does that free you from the responsibility to do what's right?

Willful blindness is a term often used in law to describe situations in which a person tries to avoid any kind of civil or criminal liability for an unlawful act by purposefully putting themselves in a position to be unaware of any facts that would render them liable. This is the church today. We don't want to take responsibility for what's going on in the world around us. Our nation is just like the man who was beaten and left for dead, and we continue to walk past on the other side of the road, ignoring the hurt.

However, by doing nothing and remaining silent on this issue, we've allowed the enemy to come in and set up camp. Our silence has allowed racism to seep down to the very roots of our culture, becoming a learned habit and a generational curse.

We have an obligation as Christians to fight for what is right, help the helpless, and love the unlovable. It's who we are called to be. It's time we step up, stop choosing blindness, and reach out to a bleeding world. Break the silence, and boldly proclaim victory over racism.

CHAPTER 13

BROTHERS IN CHRIST

I had an interesting experience several years ago while I was in revival with a dear friend of mine, Pastor Mike, who happens to be Caucasian. By the time the revival ended at that church, a pastor in a neighboring town had heard about the move of God going on and asked if we would hold a revival at his church. Naturally, we were excited to see God's people so hungry, and we eagerly agreed.

Both Mike and I had spoken to the pastor over the phone before the revival began. He told us his congregation had been thrilled when he announced it, and they were expecting great things.

On the way to the church, Mike and I were talking about the things of the Lord, getting built up in the Spirit, and making plans for who was going to preach on which nights. By the time we arrived, I practically bounded out of the vehicle, ready to get my preach on! It was like fire shut up in my bones!

The pastor greeted us outside, enthusiastically embraced Mike, and expressed his eagerness for the service. Then Mike turned and introduced me as the other preacher who would be speaking.

The pastor's face immediately fell, and he looked completely shocked. After a moment, he regained his composure and said to me, "I'm so sorry, I didn't realize you were black."

At first I was speechless. How do you respond to a statement like that? I definitely hadn't been prepared for it. Finally, when I found my voice again I asked, "Does it matter?"

"Well, not to me," he replied. "But this is a very racist area, and I just don't think my congregation will receive a black preacher."

He went on to say that he couldn't allow me to preach for fear of how his congregation would react. He was, no doubt, concerned that if he let me preach, his congregation might vote him out.

I'm not going to lie, his words hurt me. I felt like I'd been slapped in the face. Here I was all jazzed up and ready to preach, and then he tells me I can't because of the color of my skin. Talk about feeling dejected.

Mike spoke up. He told the pastor if I couldn't preach, then he wouldn't be preaching either. He went on to say we were brothers—a team—and he couldn't have one without the other.

Let me tell you, at that moment I went from feeling singled out to an overwhelming sense of love and brotherhood. Having Mike back me up like that meant more to me that I can say.

The pastor, of course, was a nervous wreck, his worry written plainly on his face. He'd advertised the revival all over town. He couldn't just call it off. Eventually, he agreed to have Mike preach that night, and when he was finished, he would let me get up and testify. If the congregation received me well, he would allow me to preach the following night.

That night after Mike finished preaching, they set up a little podium for me, and I began to testify and read a few Scriptures. Not long after I started, the crowd clapped enthusiastically and shouted, "Amen!" People were smiling and taking in everything I said.

Then the pastor caught my eye. He too was smiling and he mouthed for me to go ahead and preach. I looked at Mike, who smiled and gave me a thumbs up.

Emboldened by their encouragement, I went on to preach a whole sermon, which the people received without a second thought. That night began the greatest revival I had been in up to that time. God's spirit flowed into that church and powerful things took place there.

The first thing I want to discuss in regard to this story is the pastor. It's easy to see him as the villain in this story, but that's simply not true. Although the news he delivered did hurt, I respected him for his honesty.

Without honesty, we can never move toward healing; it's the first step. He could easily have let me preach without knowing what I was going to say and hoped for the best. Instead, he was straightforward with me, and I appreciated that. Also, I would like to mention that the pastor had no ill intent toward me. He only showed concern. And finally, he had the courage to gamble on me with his livelihood at stake. That took some real bravery on his part. He too is a hero in this story, not the bad guy. Satan is the only one at fault here.

Secondly, I want to point out Mike's behavior when presented with this situation. He could have reacted very differently and distanced himself from me. It would have been easier for him to go ahead with the revival without me. Or he could have told the pastor that he would come alone at another time. However, Mike stayed true, not only to our friendship, but to his ethics. He supported me even in the face of adversity, standing beside me no matter what the cost. That, my friends, is how it should be among the brethren. That is God's love.

> *"And in exercising godliness develop brotherly affection,*
> *and in exercising brotherly affection develop Christian love.*
> *For as these qualities are yours and increasingly abound in*
> *you, they will keep you from being idle or unfruitful unto*
> *the full personal knowledge of our Lord Jesus Christ.*
> *For whoever lacks these qualities is blind, spiritually short-*
> *sighted, seeing only what is near to him, and has become*
> *oblivious to the fact that he was cleansed from his old sins."*
>
> –1 Peter 1:7-9

This story is the perfect example of the *brotherly affection* this Scripture talks about. This particular passage stresses the importance of such love between the children of God, saying that without that love, we are blind and unfruitful.

The reality is that we *need* one another. We should support one another in weakness and defend one another in adversity. That's how God intended the Church to function. Remember who you are in God.

Though we are many different races, we have become one people. We are brothers and sisters through the bloodline of Christ. So, if you see a brother or sister hurting, have the courage and love to stand with them, and let them know they are not alone.

CHAPTER 14

CHOOSE HEALING

Almost thirty years ago, I was invited to be a guest speaker at a church in southern Missouri. As I stood in the foyer waiting for the service to begin, a little girl and her mother came through the front door.

As soon as she saw me, the little girl became excited and asked her mother, "Is that the nigger who is preaching today?"

Both the girl's mother and I stood aghast, rooted to the spot in shock. But the little girl, oblivious to the situation, ran over and hugged me enthusiastically. She then took me by the hand, and swung it back and forth, smiling at me as though we had been friends forever. It was clear to me then that there was no malice in her words, and it wasn't meant to be derogatory. The girl was merely repeating what she had heard.

In the meantime, her mother had recovered and ran over to the girl. She grabbed the girls by the arm, jerked her back, and slapped her mouth. The girl immediately started screaming and crying, unable to figure out why she was in trouble. The mother scolded her daughter, telling her to never use that word again. Then she turned to me and apologized profusely.

The woman quickly excused herself, and took the little girl back to her vehicle. I followed her outside, and reached her car just as she was putting it in gear.

She rolled down her window, apologizing again, saying how embarrassed she was.

I assured her that I wasn't offended; the girl clearly didn't mean anything by it.

She explained to me that her husband frequently used that word, despite her protestations, and that was where the girl had picked it up.

Once again, I assured her I was not offended and asked her to come back in. However, she was reluctant, wondering how the people would treat her after hearing what her daughter had said. Finally, she promised to think about it and I returned inside.

Later in the service, about the time I started to preach, they both come in and take a seat on the back row. This pleased me so much.

Toward the end of the service the woman came forward and asked me to pray for God to work a change in her husband's heart because he was, in fact, racist, though she was not. God was able to take a situation that could have easily ended with hurt and hatred and turned into a story of victory. The woman and her daughter returned each night of the revival, and God moved mightily in that place.

There are two points that I would like to make with this story. First, I want to talk about offense. Paul tells us in Acts 24:16:

> *"Herein do I exercise myself, to have always a conscience void of offense toward God, and toward men."*

As Christians, we must constantly guard against offense. This is vitally important. Offense is one of the greatest tools of the enemy, and the one we most often fall prey to. Had I not allowed God's love to lead me that night, things could have turned out very differently. I could have allowed anger and offense into my heart and carried it with me into the service. Had that happened, it would have hindered the flow of God in that service.

I could have easily lashed out in anger and said something hurtful to the woman and her daughter. My words would have caused them pain, and they would have carried that hurt home. Then perhaps she would have adopted her husband's point of view. Where would the hurt have ended? Would it have ended at all? But instead of being offended, I allowed God's love to flow through me, and He brought healing to the situation.

The second point I want to bring up is that of unfair judgment. The woman almost didn't come back into the church for fear of what others might think of her. She was not racist, though those who heard the exchange were likely to have assumed that she was. However, those who judged were the ones in sin, not the woman. Neither the woman nor her child should have been judged for the sins of her husband.

Psalm 82:2 shows us where God asks:

"How long will ye judge unjustly…"

If this woman had allowed the judgment of others to affect her decision, there couldn't have been healing.

In this situation, the opportunity for hurt and offense came from every angle. The enemy attacked on both sides. His intention was to destroy the work God was trying to do. And yet, he was overcome because we let the love of God direct our reactions.

As you go through your day, I hope you remember this story and are able to avoid falling into this trap. I encourage you to choose healing instead of hurt.

CHAPTER 15

REPENTANCE BRINGS HEALING

I n all of history, the only person to live a life free from sin was Jesus. He is the only man who never had to ask the Father for forgiveness. Since the fall of Adam, every human being who has lived on this earth has sinned. It's true. Past or present we've all done it, and we will likely sin in the future. Romans 3:23 says:

"For all have sinned and come short of the glory of God."

I have sinned. You have sinned. Ignoring this part won't make it disappear. In fact, it will only leave it room to grow. It's critical that we acknowledge our sins, ask forgiveness for them, and make a real effort to change. Only then can we move toward healing.

However, it's sometimes easier to see the fault in someone else's life than to examine our own. Matthew 7:3 says:

"And why beholdest thou the mote that is in the brother's eye, but considerest not the beam that is in thine own eye?"

Before we can begin to root out racism in the body, we must first examine our own hearts and deal with any past heartache that may be hindering the plan God has for us. 1 Peter 4:17 states:

"The time has come that judgement must begin at the house of God..."

All too often, we're too busy judging our brothers and sisters to notice sin creeping into our lives. Instead of guarding our own gates, we're busy trying to tear down the people around us. While our attention is diverted and we're concentrating on someone else's problems, Satan is setting up shop in our homes. We need to focus on weeding the enemy out of our own lives so that we can move forward.

Sin isn't something we like to acknowledge in ourselves. Sometimes it's painful or maybe even embarrassing. It's always easier to see the changes that need to be made in other's lives, rather than look at our own. However, sin is like a sickness, and ignoring it won't make it go away. It will only fester and grow if left unchecked. As I've said before, as Christians, we must constantly examine ourselves, checking our thoughts and actions against the Word of God so we don't fall prey to this trap. Satan will continually try to sneak into your camp. He's always seeking to bring you down. You have to stay on guard.

1 Corinthians 13:5 says it like this:

> *"Examine and test and evaluate your
> own selves to see whether you are holding to your faith and
> showing the proper fruits of it. Test and prove yourselves.
> Do you not yourselves realize and know thoroughly by an
> ever-increasing experience that Jesus Christ is in you—unless
> you are counterfeits disapproved on trial and rejected."*

Examining yourself allows you to recognize when and where you've failed and then repent. What does it mean to repent? Dictionary. reference.com defines it as *feeling such sorrow for a sin or fault as to be disposed to change one's life for the better.* In other words, it means to turn from what you were doing and go the other way.

Once you confess your sin and repent, you can align yourself with the heart of God, and begin operating in His love. Then that love spills over, spills out, and spills on everyone you come into contact with. Instead of causing injury, pain, or suffering, you move toward healing.

Acknowledging sin in your life is the first step. Only when sin is confessed and forsaken can fellowship be restored and enjoyed. Admitting there is a problem and confessing that sin to God will lead to reformation and restoration. 1 John 1:9 says:

"If we confess our sins, He is faithful and just to forgive us our sins, and to cleanse us from all unrighteousness."

Here's the important part, *if* we confess our sin. Sometimes it's difficult to put our pride aside and admit that we've done wrong. But the truth is, we all have. Forgiveness is something you have to ask for. God isn't a dictator; He won't force forgiveness on you. It's a gift and all you have to do is ask.

So ask yourself this: Is there hatred and racism in your own life? The answer may be more complicated than you think. Racism can take many forms. It can be either seen—as in cases where violence and verbal abuse are present—or unseen—where the sin occurs in the heart and mind without any outward sign. Racial stereotypes have become so prevalent in our current culture that many people judge others without malicious intent. And people judge not just according to race, but also by social class and gender.

Maybe you've never been mean or degrading to a person of another race, but have judged them in your mind, automatically assuming something about them because of their race. Or perhaps you hate those whose race is different from your own, though you never speak your hatred aloud. Whether or not there is physical manifestation, it is still sin.

The Bible tells us in 1 Samuel 16:7:

"...for the Lord seeth not as man seeth; for man looketh on the outward appearance, but the Lord looketh on the heart."

God looks on the heart. What will He see in yours? Is there hatred, judgment, resentment, and unforgiveness? Or will He see a heart that is molded after His own? Consider what He may find there. If you are not happy with what you find, change it.

Having said all of that, it's essential to examine yourself and make sure your heart is right before you try to help bring healing to others.

We can't help others while we are personally broken. Why? Because if you don't, you'll carry your own sin into the situation, therefore making things worse instead of better. Matthew 15:14 warns us about this, saying:

> *"They are blind guides and teachers. And if a blind man leads a blind man, both will fall into the ditch."* AMP

Checking our own hearts can prevent this from happening. If you are carrying these sins around instead of dealing with them, you are allowing them to come between you and God. The flow has been cut off, and you are no longer operating under His influence. God is the only one who can heal this situation. The only way you can help effect change is by Him working through you. Repenting of your sin and removing it from your life reopens that connection between you and the Father. When we remove sin, we adopt the mindset of God. And when you have the mindset of God, you'll find your perception changed. Hatred and hurt will be replaced by love and forgiveness. You will find a peace that passes all understanding.

Let go of your sins and let God restore you. You'll be glad you did.

CHAPTER 16

LET MERCY REIGN

No matter how many times we sin, no matter how many times we go against God, He still forgives us. Every single time. He never turns us away or tries to hurt us like we've hurt Him. No, he welcomes us back with open arms. If we look at the heart of God, we see that he delights in mercy and takes no pleasure in the death of the wicked.

Micah 7:18 says it like this:

> *"Who is a God like unto thee, that pardoneth iniquity, and passeth by the transgression of the remnant of his heritage? He retaineth not his anger forever, because he delighteth in mercy."*

God is slow to anger and abounds in lovingkindness. He's like the father in the story of the prodigal son. That father welcomed his son home without a second thought or even a hint of an accusation. He was simply overjoyed to have his son back.

Like that father, God never holds our past sins over our heads or reminds us of our past failings. All He wants is to love us and for us to love Him.

Unfortunately, we forget about the mercy that has been afforded to us when it comes to dealing with others. We want mercy for our own sins but are unwilling to dole it out where our brothers and sisters are concerned. We feel justified in our wrath, believing it's our right.

However, the Bible tells us differently. In James 1:10 it says:

*"The anger of man does not produce
the righteousness of God."*

Anger never makes anything better, nor does it do anything to further the Kingdom. We know this, but instead of mercy-motivated prayers, we pray for the judgment of our enemies. Why? Because we let our anger control our actions.

The Bible tells us in Luke 6:36:

"Be ye therefore merciful, as your Father also is merciful."

However, the Church today is severely lacking in this area. Instead of a refuge for the broken, we've become a hanging tree for the fallen. We're not here to fulfill God's wrath, but to complete His mercy. The Church is supposed to be a house of prayer for all nations, but instead we're a house of judgment. When will we step up and become what we are destined to be?

Even non-Christians have heard the story of Sodom. In Abraham's time, it was one of the wickedest cities in the world. Sin ran rampant, and they were godless people. Because of the evil residing there, God was going to destroy it.

"And the Lord said, 'because the cry of Sodom and Gomorrah is great, and because their sin is very grievous; I will go down now, and see whether they have done altogether according to the cry of it, which is come unto me; and if not, I will know.' And the men turned their faces from thence, and went toward Sodom: but Abraham stood yet before the Lord."

–Genesis 18:20-22

When presented with the possibility of Sodom's annihilation, Abraham didn't jump on the bandwagon to destroy it. Instead, he was moved by mercy. He choose to look through the eyes of compassion, and saw something he thought could be saved. And when all the other men had left, Abraham still stood, pleading with the Lord.

> *"And Abraham drew near, and said, Wilt thou also destroy the righteous with the wicked? Peradventure there be fifty righteous within the city: wilt thou also destroy and not spare the place for the fifty righteous that are therein? That be far from thee to do after this manner, to slay the righteous with the wicked: and that the righteous should be as the wicked that be far from thee: Shall not the Judge of all the earth do right?"*
>
> –Genesis 18:23-25

God answered, saying that if he found even fifty people, he would spare the city. Abraham then asked God if He would spare the city if He only found forty-five righteous people. He kept going, asking about thirty, then twenty, and finally ten people, to which God agreed. Abraham's mercy-motivated prayer had grabbed the heart of God. Abraham could've easily stepped aside and let all those who were in the city perish. Instead, he stood before the Lord and begged for mercy on behalf of the people so they wouldn't be destroyed. The world could use more people like Abraham—merciful men and women who wish to see people redeemed instead of destroyed.

Because of God's deal with Abraham, He couldn't destroy the city as long as righteous people dwelt there. He sent angels into the city to warn and evacuate Lot—who was a righteous man—and his family.

We see in Genesis 19:22 were God's hand was stayed because of Lot:

> *"Hasten thee, escape thither; for I cannot do anything till thou come thither...."*

As long as Lot remained in the city, judgment could not come.

Where are the men and women of God who will stand in the gap for those who have fallen? How soon we forget that Jesus stands in the gap for us. We need to position ourselves between the failings of men and the wrath of God, praying for mercy on others' behalf and stay there until total transformation comes. Instead we look down on them in judgment like the Pharisees of old, unforgiving and cynical, habitually doubting the possibility of their redemption.

Mercy is a lesson Job had an intimate understanding of. At a time in his life when Job was at his worst—having lost everything: his wealth, his lands, his family, and finally his health—his three closest friends stopped by. Naturally, he thought they were there to comfort him. However, they began to mock him instead. Even his wife told him to curse God and die. Just when he needed them most, they turned against him. He had every reason to hate them, to pray for their misfortune. However, when God's anger was kindled against them, He spared them because Job was praying for mercy. Job's prayers saved them. We're supposed to pray mercifully, not vindictively.

Jesus often stressed to His disciples the importance of mercy, instructing them in Matthew 5:44 to:

> *"Love your enemies, bless them that curse you,*
> *do good to them that hate you, and pray for them*
> *which despitefully use you, and persecute you."*

What are we but disciples? The same rules that applied to the twelve disciples still apply to us today. When people mistreat us, we're to show mercy.

Ezekiel 22:30 tells us that God looks for people who will stand in the gap:

> *"And I sought for a man among them, that should*
> *make up the hedge, and stand in the gap before me for the*
> *land, that I should not destroy it: but I found none."*

I would hate to think that He could find no one willing to pray for mercy. It's heartbreaking to even think about. What if I was the one in need of mercy, and no one could be found to pray? What if we had no one to stand in for us?

The Bible says in Hebrews 7:25 that Jesus:

*"Is able to save to the uttermost them
that draw near unto God through him, seeing he
ever liveth to make intercession for them."*

He is constantly praying for us, asking mercy of the Father. But what if he stopped? What if He decided we were no longer worth it? Can you even image? And yet we still withhold mercy from those who need it most.

James 5:16 says:

*"Confess your faults one to another, and pray
one for another, that ye may be healed. The effectual
fervent prayer of a righteous man availeth much."*

So let's pray for each other instead of hating each other. Let's move toward healing.

Dwight L. Moody (who founded Moody Bible Institute in 1886) once said, "When we preach on hell, we might at least do it with tears in our eyes." Hell is a horrible place. I wouldn't wish it on my worst enemy.

I want to challenge you. Next time someone hurts you, instead of reacting in anger, react with mercy. If we all do this, I believe that we'll start to see major change in our world. So instead of letting anger rule, let mercy reign.

CHAPTER 17

LET GO AND LET GOD

I remember being invited to preach at a weeklong conference in Kentucky some years ago. The pastor of the church had recently been appointed when he contacted me about speaking. He explained that he had already scheduled a speaker for every night but Friday, and asked if I would take the slot and finish out the revival. I eagerly agreed, glad to be a part of it.

The days were counting down, the revival getting closer. I was preparing my sermon and getting excited about the message God had given me. Thursday, the day before I was supposed to preach, I received a phone call from the pastor. At the insistence of his wife, he had called to let me know exactly what I was coming in to. He went on to explain that his deacons had unanimously supported the revival when he proposed it.

That is, until he mentioned that there would be a black man preaching on Friday. At that point one of his deacons stood up from the table and very angrily proclaimed that no black man would ever preach in that church while he was a deacon.

Racism, the pastor informed me, was still very much alive and quite prominent in that area. However, he let me know that he had no problem risking his newly acquired pastorate to have me preach. As long as I felt okay with coming, he would support me.

Now logically, I probably should have been a little concerned about my safety. In my heart, though, I knew God had called me to this meeting; and if He had called me, I knew I was safe.

The gentleman whom I was traveling with, however, was less than convinced. He begged me to take some kind of protection, but I declined.

I knew that giving in to fear and carrying a weapon would only cause more tension and would make a potentially bad situation so much worse.

Finally, the night came for me to preach, and the house was packed out. We had an awesome service, and many came up for prayer afterward.

In the middle of praying for people, I noticed several of the deacons had pulled the pastor to the side, and were engaged in some sort of discussion. I'm not going to lie; it made me a little nervous. At first I tried to ignore them, but I wondered if trouble was brewing. What if the disgruntled deacon was demanding that the pastor throw me out? It was bothering me to the point of distraction, so I finally went over and asked the pastor what was going on.

He smiled and told me his deacons wanted to ask me to stay on and preach an extra night.

I tell you, I was both ecstatic and more than a little relieved. I had been expecting the worst. So I said to the pastor, "What about that one deacon? The one that didn't want me to come?"

He smiled at me, pointed across the room, and said, "That's him laying over there in the floor. You prayed with him a few minutes ago."

I was amazed! I had no idea who he was when he came up for prayer. I was so blessed to find out that he was able to see past his hatred, and accept me as his brother in Christ. He found me after service and hugged me, apologizing as he wept. Praise the Lord! What an awesome example of God's love changing lives! Instead of hurt, reformation broke through.

Sometimes we just have to let go of our hurts, follow God's direction—even if it's a little scary—and let Him do the rest. Things could have been drastically different from how they turned out. If that young pastor hadn't been obedient and willing to take a chance with me, or had I let fear keep me from that meeting, that deacon's life would have never been changed in such a radical way.

Many times I have been the victim of racism, but in letting God direct my reaction, I have overcome it. As I have said before, racism is a problem that can only be fixed through God. Let go of the hurt, and let God take the reins. He can tear down any racial barriers if we just let Him.

You don't have to try to change anyone, only love them as God would. His love will change them.

CHAPTER 18

A FATHER'S WISDOM

As I look back on my life, I see so many things I'm thankful for. The love and wisdom of my parents, a wonderful family, and good friends, just to name a few. However, sometimes it's easy to take for granted the people who have been divinely placed in our lives. God sets certain people in place to shape you and mold you throughout the course of your life.

For me, one of those people was my father. He was a powerful role model and a wise man. I honor him for so many reasons. Not only was he a provider, protector, and corrector, but he also gave us direction and taught us how to walk in the ways that were good and just. My father showed me by his own example that just because you grew up in a mess doesn't mean you have to come out smelling like it. Despite all the terrible things my father had to deal with in his life, my father was steadfast in his beliefs. He always taught us to honor and respect those around us, especially those in authority.

My father grew up in a time when racism was at an all-time high. It was a challenging time in African-American history. Blacks were grossly mistreated, yet this was the accepted behavior of the day. Segregation was in full swing. Blacks were made to sit in the back of buses—if they were allowed to sit at all. The common practice was to make a black person stand so that a white person could have his or her seat. Signs were clearly displayed in windows and on the walls of business stating that they were "White Only" vendors. Or if a business did serve blacks, they had to stand outside and wait for their food so as not to offend the white patrons. Blacks were charged the same price but not allowed the same privileges.

Those were trying times, and injustice was rampant. People were afraid to speak out against such inequality and mistreatment for fear of losing their own lives.

My father dealt with all of this and more in his time. Yet, despite it all, he never wavered from his righteous standard and remained steadfast in his faith. He never let all of the pain, hidden hurts, dehumanizing, and disrespectful acts break his spirit or change his character. Like so many others, my father could have easily given into the torments of life and become bitter and jaded, but he didn't. Not only that, but he shielded his family from it. Regardless of my father's brushes with racism, he refused to join in the hatred.

I can never express how grateful I am that my father had such wisdom in this matter. He could have easily introduced that poisonous hatred into our lives . . . could have turned us against white people. Instead, he taught us to honor, love, respect, and to try to get along with everyone. He taught us to forgive those who did us wrong and not to hold grudges.

You've heard the saying, "If someone throws you a lemon, fill it with sugar, and hand it back to them as lemonade." If they flip you off, add another finger and make it a peace sign. Don't let the actions of others affect your character. That's what my father taught me.

I would like to thank my father for his wisdom, for not letting his experiences leave him bitter and for not bringing that bitterness into our lives and tainting our perceptions of the world.

Because of him, I can see people of all races and social rank as human beings. I can see the beautiful diversity as God intended and treat people as such. Thank you, Daddy, for having the courage to stand for what is good and just in a world where so few would. You're my number one hero.

CHAPTER 19

DO THE RIGHT THING

I recently had the pleasure of watching *The Blind Side*, starring Sandra Bullock. I was so moved by this story and the message it gives. The film is based on the incredible true story of Michael Oher. In the movie, Michael is a young black man who is homeless. His mother is a cocaine addict, and he doesn't even know who his father is. Mike is alone, traumatized, and without many options. That is, until he meets a white couple named Leigh Anne and Sean Tuohy. They take Mike into their home and give him food, clothes, and a place to call home. Not only that, but they go above and beyond, making sure Michael was given every chance and tool he needed to succeed.

The movie moved me to tears more than once. The whole time I was watching, I was sitting there thinking, *this is how it should be!* The color of your skin shouldn't matter. The only thing that should matter is whether it's the right thing to do.

My heart was so stirred by this movie that it brought back memories from my own past. I recall a time over twenty years ago that I was able to help save a life. As I drove home from work one evening, I suddenly heard a woman scream. Following the sound, I saw a young white girl being brutally beaten by her ex-boyfriend, a young black man. Her terrified screams and bloodied face spurred me into action.

My instinct to protect and do the right thing kicked in, and I jumped out of my car with the engine still running and ran over to help. Blood dripped from her nose, mouth, and ears. The force of his punch had been so great that I actually heard her jaw break as I ran to assist her.

I quickly put myself between the young lady and her attacker, shoving him back and giving him a few terse words. He finally backed off and ran to his car to get away.

In the meantime, another lady had stopped to help and called 911. Together we were able to dress some of the girl's wounds and wash her up a little while we waited for the EMTs. They immediately rushed her off to the hospital where they performed emergency surgery to repair her broken jaw. In the end, she had to have some facial reconstruction and her jaws were wired shut.

The next day, I stopped by the hospital to check on the young lady. Her family and friends greeted me with hugs and tears of thanks for saving her life. It didn't matter to them that I was a black man any more than it mattered to me that the young lady was white. What mattered was that I knew what was right and acted accordingly. I could have driven by like I didn't see anything, chosen to not get involved. However, because I stopped, a life was saved.

When the time comes for you to make a decision, always chose to do the right thing. Whether that means giving someone a ride, feeding the hungry, or even giving shelter to those who need it. It doesn't matter who needs our help or what color their skin is; we should always be willing to extend a helping hand.

Just the willingness to help goes a long way. Remember, you could be in their shoes one day and could be the one who needs help. You may need someone else's prayer, encouragement, strength, wisdom, or direction. Keep in mind that when that time comes, the person who helps the most may not be the race or skin tone you prefer, but they will be exactly who you need.

When you're going through a crisis, things like race don't matter. If you're having a heart attack, you don't stop to think about what nationality your surgeon is. All that matters is that he's fixing the problem. Or if someone breaks into your home, you don't ask for a police officer of a specific race. All you want is help, no matter the form. It's time that we start acting on what is right, not what is easy. When it's the right thing to do, do the right thing.

The End of Racism

Throughout these pages I've discussed every facet of racism, from hatred to hurt and sin to forgiveness. I've shared some of my own personal struggles and victories, as well as historical facts, and biblical truths. So where do we stand at the end of all of this? It is my sincere hope that we stand together, united against racism and all the fruits thereof.

Ending racism is not a task we can complete alone. We can only accomplish this by allowing God to work through us. However, as a nation, we have turned our back on God. We were once a God-fearing nation founded on morals and biblical truths. That is no longer the case. It seems as though we've turned those beliefs on their heads, and thumbed our noses at the principles of God. In the name of free speech, we spew hatred and injustice over the airways, promoting dissension and unrest. We murder thousands of unborn children every year saying that it our right to choose. We are a society in love with profane acts and sexual immorality. Pornography and profanity are accepted, calling it freedom of expression. Our schools are no longer a safe place for our children to learn and grow because we have removed God, and prayer is no longer allowed. We have taken the very principles that our nation was founded on, and perverted them. In our nation, what the Bible calls evil, we call good, and what the Bible calls good, we call evil. We have lost our spiritual equilibrium, tipping the scales in the wrong direction. How long will this be allowed to go on? Deuteronomy 8:20 states:

> *"As the nations which the Lord destroyeth before*
> *your face, so shall ye perish; because ye would not be*
> *obedient unto the voice of the Lord your God."*

It's time that we as a nation and as a people wake up. Our destruction is coming swiftly if we do nothing to change it. So join with me, brothers and sisters. There is still hope for America if we can return to the faith we were founded on. Let's turn this around.

You may recall the children's show, *Scooby Doo*. In the show, a group of kids and their dog investigated reports of monsters, ghouls, and ghosts. It always seemed like their foes were too great, too powerful to defeat. Every show filled you with suspense as you wondered how they would ever overcome their circumstances. However, at the end when they removed the monster's mask, it was only a man underneath. Once unmasked, the man was always handcuffed and led away by officers, no longer seeming so powerful. Racism is the same as these supposed monsters. We tend to think of racism as the undefeatable problem. However, through the course of this book we have unmasked this monster of racism that has been terrorizing our nation. The façade has been stripped away, and we can see it for what it truly is, and it doesn't scare us any longer.

Now that we can see the truth about racism, how do we get rid of it? Well, as any farmer worth his salt would tell you, in order to kill out a tough weed, you have to kill it from the root. You can't just do a surface treatment. It may look like it is dead or dying, but at the root it is still alive and well. Given time, that weed will crop back up, and be all the more difficult to deal with.

Racism is still a very prevalent issue in our nation today. You can try to hide it or downplay it, but the fact is that it still remains, the dividing line still stands. There is still very unfair and unjust treatment of minority races. They are still very often looked upon as second-class citizens, inferior to majority races. You can tell by the tensions in the media of late that we are nowhere near a resolve. This is a problem that should trouble all Americans, especially Christians. Instead we use the Bible, and twist scriptures to justify our actions, when truthfully the Bible clearly speaks against it. For instance, Genesis 1:27 says:

> *"So God created man in His own image, in the image of God created he him; male and female created He them."*

This tells us that all of mankind is the work of God, the master artist. Whether black, white, Hispanic, Asian, Arabic, or any other race, God handmade each of us. We are each precious.

Don't get me wrong, there will still be opportunity for hurt, offense, and hatred. But you have to keep the mind of God in this matter and not allow offense to color your decisions. You've heard the phrase, *"seeing the world through rose-colored glasses."* It's time that we see the world through Christ-colored glasses. Instead of looking through our physical eyes, we should only see the blood of Jesus that connects us all. There is no race within the body of Christ. The Bible gives very clear instructions on race, providing distinct direction on issues that our nation is divided over. It doesn't make distinctions based on physical appearance or social attributes. In fact, when Samuel questioned God about anointing David as king because of his physical appearance, God corrected him and told him not to judge by outward appearances. Not only that, but the Bible strongly speaks against prejudice and hatred repeatedly, and calls for reconciliation. We should treat all men and women with respect and dignity. After all, are we not are all Children of the King? God doesn't see people the same way we do. Isaiah 16:7 says that God looks on the heart. Galatians 3:28 says:

> *"There is neither Jew nor Greek, there is neither bond nor free, there is neither male nor female: for ye are all one in Christ Jesus."*

We are all the same, all brothers and sisters. If people can look past what they see on the outside, they will find a family that they didn't even know they had. I encourage all of you to try to see those around you as God sees them. Don't just judge by appearance or situation. Forgive, and love. Try to heal and help others do the same. Isn't it time that we put all of this behind us and move forward? What do you say? Let's put an end to racism by destroying it at the root so it doesn't grow back.

ABOUT THE AUTHOR

Dr. Ron Webb is the pastor of the Mt. Calvary Powerhouse Church in Poplar Bluff, Missouri. Pastor Webb has been in the ministry for over 30 years. He attended Three Rivers Community College in Poplar Bluff where he majored in Business Administration and was a former "Raider" basketball player. He earned his Bachelor of Theology degree from the International College of Bible Theology, and a Master Degree of Pastor Studies in counseling, and a Doctorate in Theology from Midwest Theological Seminary. Dr. Webb also had the honor of doing the invocation at the inauguration for Missouri Governor Jay Nixon.

The unique ministry of Dr. Ron Webb is evident as he is anointed in the areas of church leadership and governance. Dr. Webb has been considered by many to be "A Pastor to Pastors." His ministry is centered on restoration and racial reconciliation and a sincere belief that we must teach the lost at any cost. His preaching and teaching focuses on empowerment and hope.

Dr. Webb is CEO and President of *S.E.M.O. Christian Restoration Center*, a place for individuals who need a second chance in life. He is founder and lead instructor of *School of the Prophets Bible College* in Poplar Bluff, Missouri. Students leave this Bible college as trained and experienced leaders ready to fulfill Jesus' command in Matthew 28:19 to "Go ye therefore, and teach all nations."

The *Heartland Family Center,* a homeless shelter for families, is the newest outreach ministry organized and founded in 2007 by Dr. Webb, and is owned and operated by Mt. Calvary Powerhouse Church. The goal is to serve families whose circumstances have deprived them of adequate living and housing. In a Christ-like manner, families in need are provided housing and services to help them become self-sufficient.

Covenant Ministries is another ministry designed by Dr. Webb to advance God's Kingdom by providing a fellowship in which men and women of God find mutual encouragement, edification, counsel, and participation in leadership and ministerial training.

Dr. Webb is married to the lovely Georgia Webb and they have three children: Ronnie, Jr., Tony, and Jackie (Webb) Brown. Grandpa Ron and Grandma Georgia boast two grandchildren so far: Jerrell Brown, Jr. and Jaxson Brown.